Dear Chelsea Terhaar:
I'm flattered to hear
of your admiration for
my writing. Please enjoy
a story / poem or two
within. I look forward
to meeting someday...
best,
Sam Lucy
winthp +27-05'

Holding Ground

FRIENDS, BIRDS, AND THE LAND BETWEEN

SAMUEL LUCY

Camden, Maine

ISBN 0-89272-638-5

Library of Congress Control Number 2004115413

Interior and dust-jacket design by Phil Schirmer

Printed at Versa Press Inc., East Peoria, Illinois

5   4   3   2   1

Countrysport Press
Camden, Maine
A division of Down East Enterprise, publishers of
Shooting Sportsman magazine

For orders and catalog information, call 800-685-7962 or visit
www.countrysportpress.com

Table of Contents

Foreword

In my life I've known several kindred spirits—people to whom I've felt more connected than merely acquainted. The connections have ranged from shared thoughts and attitudes to common philosophies and goals, but in each person I've seen reflections of myself as I've gotten to know them over time. Sam Lucy is one of these people.

I "met" Sam in 1994, shortly after I'd moved from New York to Maine, to be the editor of *Shooting Sportsman* magazine. Sam had recently made his own move, uprooting himself from New Hampshire and settling on the opposite coast, in Washington. We were introduced when he sent me a story for consideration, one he thought would complement the magazine as much as the magazine would complement it. He was right.

That first submission was the title chapter of this book, "Holding Ground," and after reading it I was hooked. I was taken especially with the main character's thoughtfulness and emotion; the fresh, sentient descriptions; the way the writing ebbed and flowed with a comfortable, easy rhythm. But more than that there was nothing overwritten or showy, no effort made to wow the reader with a five-star vocabulary; it was simply a well-crafted story about a subject most bird hunters could relate to. It felt familiar.

In the decade since, I've received many such pieces from Sam. They've been good "reads" all, yet my appreciation for them has been deeper than story lines and style. It has been about Sam's ability to strike visceral chords, to make readers empathize with characters through shared emotions and experiences. It's writing from the heart, and the words are masterful in their simplicity.

And it's through Sam's writing that I've come to know the man. Having shaken his hand only once, I've gleaned most of my knowledge through his characters and correspondence. In reading his work, for example, it's obvious that Sam's a hunter—hard-core, in fact, and as comfortable in a duck blind as in the uplands. He's also a farmer, one who finds satisfaction in working the soil and bringing forth crops. His "day job" is as a land restorer, returning things to the way they were, with an eye toward aiding wildlife.

In addition to our shared passions for hunting and writing—and to the fact that I've always wanted to farm—my feelings of kinship with Sam stem from the parallel paths our lives have taken. I mentioned that when we first corresponded, we'd both just completed moves—though at the time Sam felt his was likely temporary. Shortly thereafter we each bought gun-dog pups, then followed up by marrying and having kids (he being blessed with two girls, I with two boys). These days we remain on opposite sides of the country and compare notes on children and graying dogs and how bird numbers are likely to be come fall. Simple things, true, but threads that link lives and provide stories for the telling.

This past year I sneaked a flock of black ducks and mallards, managing three with two shots. Afterward I thought of Sam, as I know it was the type of hunt he'd have enjoyed. Just as I've enjoyed vicariously living so many of his hunts. As for the woodcock covert in "Holding Ground," I've been there—not literally, but each time I read the story I'm taken to a valley in northern Vermont, one with a similarly riffled river, an aldered island, a pair of 'doodles twittering in at day's end. It's one I've visited with another kindred spirit, Tim Leary, who passed away—like some of Sam's closest friends—much too soon.

So when you sit down to read this book, give yourself time. Find a quiet place with soft light, and make sure the dog's curled up nearby. These are words to be savored, and they're likely to evoke

memories and emotions from seasons past. Maybe you'll wish you'd
been along for the day—or feel thankful that you weren't. But
regardless, odds are you'll connect with Sam Lucy the way I have: as
the hunters' writer he is.

Ralph P. Stuart
Editor in Chief, *Shooting Sportsman*
September 2004

Preface

Nearly thirty years ago I went on my first bird hunt. Twenty years ago I started writing about it, and about ten years ago I started to publish. It may seem preposterous that someone can be as enthralled with something after three decades, but I return to both writing and bird hunting with the same captured interest as the very first time. I believe this is simple: Each new hunt or each fresh line leads to the unknown, and there is little else in life I can say that about, with child rearing being the only possible exception.

Certainly the thrill of the hunt has changed form over that time; it's now a lot more about friendships shared and the dogs. You hear that from elders while growing up, but you truly have to hunt a while to actually feel what they meant. And it has become more about hunting in pretty places and the silence and the rawness of the birds themselves and the great celebration of eating their wild goodness than the numbers bagged.

The mystique is what first caught me, and it is what holds me to this day. The fascination of the untouchable. The reckless emotion that hits me at sunrise on a quiet marsh, at the final turn of a call-fooled drake or a convinced flock of geese, or at the sudden drum of the ruffed grouse's flush through the November woods. And surely at the twitter and teeter of the timberdoodle when I reminisce about the faraway woodcock coverts I miss.

I'm blessed to have grown up in the country and to have had parents who were so worn out with children that they allowed me to roam at will across a precious New England hill and dale. And I am blessed to now live in a completely different yet equally free-roam-ing landscape in the great Northwest. It is here that I hope to raise my own children in similar fashion, with the help of my knowing wife.

I have my father to thank for buying me my first shotgun at age twelve: a Stevens double-barrel 16-gauge that I shot my first grouse, woodcock, black duck, and goose with. And I thank my mother for having the courage to trust me in that gun's responsible use. Because of Gene Hill, my parents also bought me my first Brittany at age fourteen. It is from reading Gene's work that I started scratching away at some hunting stories of my own. My favorite and lifelong English teacher, Bob Fisher, further encouraged this indulgence.

My Uncle Thad is the one who actually took me bird hunting a few times and instilled my fever with the enthusiasm he can generate in anything. And I have to thank my few close hunting buddies for putting up with me. As well as my dogs. You know who you are. If you recognize yourself somewhere within these pages, well, too bad . . .

Not long after I made my move west, some twelve years ago now, I found myself in Dr. Robert Maves's dentist chair talking birds and dogs. Soon I had my first Lab, and Bob pointed me toward the wonderful world of waterfowl we have here in central Washington. He died suddenly and at too young an age. I regret terribly never having hunted with him. It is to the memory of Bob and to the memory of my friend Johnny Haase that this book is dedicated.

Sam Lucy
Winthrop, Washington

Coming Home

Sibyl reached the top of the plateau and saw the run of wheat stubble stretching into the late-afternoon December sun. The blinding white snow made swirling patterns where the wind had been unable to sweep it from the fields. As she took in the jagged mountains beyond, the river fog below, Sibyl felt her stomach roll because she knew she was back in her country. She'd motored straight up from Texas, and her pickup hadn't set wheels in the Northwest for seven years. At last, her mind eased. She sighed out loud and slowed the pace. Sibyl wondered how it was that she'd left this land in the first place.

It had been back and forth with Paul for a year now and December, she decided, was as good a time to leave as any. She had two grand in her pocket and only the things she'd need for winter in the north.

She had loved Paul in his country but never the land of Texas so much as this. She knew he'd find the emptiness of snow stretching before her desolate. Indeed, her father hadn't been able to keep a wife in this country, any more than her brother had. Yet Sibyl couldn't decide what she wanted to do first: head for the timbered hills behind the ranch for a powdery ski run; stand in the manure-warm horse barn and drink in the tangy odor; or dig out her shotgun, get brother Tom, and go look for Hungarian partridge, ducks, geese, or just the setting sun.

A line from Hemingway came to her and she felt herself, like Nick Adams, begin to hunt the country in her mind: the brush-choked draws leading up from the wheat into rocks and sage; the creek bed that bordered the field for miles and that never froze and would hold mallards into midwinter. Tom hadn't written her for two years after she first left. The two of them had been snowshoeing and jump-shooting ducks along this creek the day she told him she was Texas bound. His face had gone blank, and he'd told her she was foolish to move someplace just for a man.

At the time, Tom's wife had just left him, saying the open white ate her guts out. He proclaimed he wasn't leaving the country for anything. Everyplace else would only crowd him, he said, and he had a ranch to run. Sibyl marveled at how he'd stayed his course, while she herself had taken flight. Her father had finally found another wife and left for Alberta. Sibyl had almost mocked Tom's resistance and stubbornness, but now, for the first time, she wavered toward understanding.

She pulled her pickup to the side of the road, got out, and put on her watch cap, mittens, and parka. She opened the truck canopy and dug through her belongings till she found a bottle of red wine there. Sibyl took out the bottle and held it to the sinking sun so that the wine made a blood red sky, a spilled-on land, then she pulled the cork and drank very slowly till she could feel the wine run all through her.

A flock of snowbirds descended upon the road to pick gravel. A lone eagle soared over the wheat and stretched up against distant peaks that cut the horizon like a saw. Sibyl would love nobody in this country—nobody for a while, and she might or might not move on. She didn't feel all bitter inside; she'd only grown hard during the drive in order to get on with the going. Her hands were still rough from the digging in Texas. It was the first time she'd been in real wool mittens for what seemed like forever; she had happily bought them on her way through Colorado.

A breeze tried now and then, but the land lay mostly still. It was a rare day as such, the kind that came either right before a storm or right after. Sibyl noticed where Hungarian partridge had scratched at the field edge, trying for wheat seed below the snow. There was no sign of geese using the field, and she saw only a single set of deer tracks.

Tom had lost his wife but now had another Lab which, in a letter to Sibyl, he considered a fair trade. Sibyl wondered how he was doing with the dog. She wondered if the rise in grain prices was allowing Tom more time to ride, hunt, and read—all the things he loved most.

She wanted to ride horseback after the partridge, letting strong legs reach out across the open the way he'd taught her to ride—free and easy to the rhythm of the beast below, till the threat of saddle sores no longer existed. It was the same way she, in turn, had taught Paul to ride the desert lands, but it never was the way it was with Tom, in new snow, scouting for the next day's hunt. Here the air snapped at night, sunrise flooded the land with mist and gold, and they oiled their guns by the woodstove in the early dawn before barn chores, the perfumery smell of solvent filling the kitchen.

And Sibyl could see what came later: the dog working the snow, its tail beginning to go in circles as it tightened the back-and-forth movement that drew her and Tom to attention. Then there would be the sudden rush of wings, sometimes too far away to shoot, sometimes right at their feet. The close flushes were the best, when they had time to recover and pick out a bird from the covey and swing to it till nothing in the world existed except the full gray and red of the Hun against a white land. Then there was the follow-through, the pulling of the trigger once, twice. And how the world would go still after a connection was made. First came the moment of remorse, then the moment of reward as the dog brought back a perfectly put-together thing, its warmth and rarity filling her pocket as they moved on.

You could only love a person so much, Sibyl thought, whereas you could float across and love the land in new and different ways every time you touched down. You could even love it without touching down. It was the cause for your rising, your drifting, your ungrounded yet completely grounded compassion for all things of truth and strength, be it the coyote standing patient for winter mice, or a covey of Huns crowding shoulder to shoulder and plowing up a

patch of foot-deep snow till they could get at autumn's treasures preserved beneath.

Sibyl studied the hastening sun through the wine again and wondered what Tom's reaction would be when she sneaked up on the
kitchen window, the barn, his truck, or wherever she found him. He
hadn't a clue she was home; she'd had no idea she was coming. Maybe
she would go to the woodshed and see if any fresh game hung there,
just as she used to do when first home from school on autumn and
early-winter afternoons. To see if Tom had hung the birds she liked so
much to feel: the smooth, light feathers of Huns and grouse; the thick,
heavy down of winter mallards and Canada geese.

Sibyl would later make holiday wreaths from those feathers—and
pillows with the down. And she learned the best way to roast the birds
in marmalade sauce and apple and garden onion, the way that her
father and Tom enjoyed so much they'd go on and on with their rav-
ing. It was nearly enough to cure the cold emptiness behind their
mother's leaving, her abrupt abandonment, her sudden and lasting disappearance. Till they read about her in the Sioux Falls newspaper that
their cousins sent after the funeral.

Sibyl raised the bottle of wine, took a hand from its mitten and
smoothed back her long, sandy hair. She wiped at the hard memories
of her mother, who'd raised her into puberty with such tenderness
then left for no known reason. The mother whose disappearance only
became eased by her death. Sibyl would never forget, especially
around Christmas, yet she was left with what she was left with.

Paul, her Texas love, had been most compassionate about Sibyl's
mom. Sibyl wiped, too, at the memory of Paul. Which way to forgive-
ness, she wondered.

Then she began skiing the country in her mind. She could hear the
hiss of varnished wood cutting snow as she strode out across the
wheat and headed for the foothills in back of the ranch. There she'd
climb through the timber to her favorite open glade, which she'd
named Susie after her best high-school friend, who'd also quit this

country. It was in that glade, in winter, where she'd become most interested in rocks one day while skiing. She'd found a perfect broad-leafed fossil stuck in the side of a boulder—a leaf-print from the vegetation of some long-ago time, one she couldn't possibly imagine.

Not originally planning on college, that fast Sibyl developed an interest outside the ranch. She tightened her grades, got some scholarship money through her agricultural background, and went off to college in the eastern part of the state. She returned to the ranch summers to help out her brother and father. Then, during her senior year, she was invited on a fossil dig in Texas and was soon gone for seven years.

She could feel her wooden skis start down past that fossil rock, the easiness of light powder holding her gently around the knees as she swooped bird-like in turn after bending turn, through evergreens and snow. Maybe she would go skiing first, after all. Her stomach swirled as it did when Paul was deep inside her under quiet desert-night skies with nothing but the sound of their own breath in gulps. Some things, it seemed, were in her more than others, but the skiing would at least soothe her with the sharp, red touch of winter on her face.

She would be back to the ranch at dusk: the glow of orange light in the horse barn at chore time, the smell of the cattle, the feeling of the woodstove and hot tea and rich cooking that she and Tom would get to after the horses and cattle were fed, and the stove was stoked.

Sibyl didn't want to miss December dusk at the ranch, so she corked up the wine after one more swallow. She climbed back into her pickup and started driving toward the setting sun, now making the sky bloody all of its own. The warmth inside her grew the closer to the ranch she drove. Soon she was at the turn onto the half-mile drive across the creek and up to the house.

Right there at the turn, Sibyl spotted them: thirty Huns huddled in a circle, scrounging for food. Though it was too dark now to detect color, she envisioned their rust-colored heads and powdery gray breast feathers, their winter plumpness puffed up against the cold. She couldn't wait to tell Tom.

Sibyl crossed the creek and then could see the lights of the horse barn. She could see the great shape of the old combine, parked in the snow like a lost dinosaur in a bare field: the long spout, the huge, monolithic head. Next to it was the three-ton dump truck. Still, these remained the tools of the trade, and Sibyl felt herself in late-summer harvest, the chaff blowing down her neck as she rode the combine with her father over fields of untouched wheat, Tom driving the truck as the combine filled it with the year's planting. She remembered the hot sun, the noise, and then the excitement around figuring just how many bushels per acre they'd come up with.

The lean years of low prices, drought, or flood; the bitter debates between father, son, and wife over whether to sell or not were well behind Sibyl at the moment. She only thought of Tom's face when she entered the barn and just how long he'd try to act nonchalant before lifting her high into the air. She wondered if he'd bothered to get a Christmas tree, whether he had hope left in this world. Their mother had always made it a point to drop all else during Christmastime. If Tom hadn't gotten a tree, they would go out and get one together as they used to and carry it in on horseback so as to keep it perfect.

As Sibyl made the final approach to the ranch, the barn lights went out and the yard light revealed a tall figure heading for the woodshed with two large shapes hanging from one arm. "Geese for Christmas," she whispered. "Good going, Tom."

For the first time in a long while, Sibyl recognized her feelings. She understood this land. She wanted to ride and hunt this country on and on. And she felt, right then, that the best—the very best—part about coming home was this moment, just before.

Shoeing Otter Bog

Jake's Lab sniffed the snowshoes where they stood leaning against the wood bin and seemed to approve. Jake knew where the shoes would take him, knew the place he'd built them for as he studied their lacquered finish in the cabin firelight. He smiled, realizing how much easier the shoes would make it for both him and the dog. He felt smug at the simple notion that such a place as Otter Bog existed. And, of course, at the fact that he alone hunted it.

Otter Bog never froze; even at minus thirty, the warm springs added enough flow so the pungent water shed ice like a thick winter beard. Like Jake's blond beard when ice formed along its edges but never penetrated the middle, the beard that he now stroked methodically as he rocked in satisfaction, half-sleepy in front of the stove.

The bog in its entirety was a series of small beaver ponds linked by a quarter-mile of grassy creek. Two main bodies of water lay on either end. It was a mile's walk from the toolshed where a neighboring farmer had given Jake permission to park. The trip was always an easy walk on bare ground in the early fall but not so easy in three feet of fresh snow. It left a man wet enough after he finally got to water that he couldn't stay long despite layers of thick wool. And snow had been falling for over a month now, having started the first of November.

That April, Jake had hung two straight ash saplings that his Colville Native friend had gotten from the north section of the reservation. Come October, Jake cut the ash to a pattern his friend showed him, then began hewing the wood, smoothing it, soaking it, and finally bending the two resulting pieces into a suitable, toe-lifted shape. After he laid the cross braces, he began stringing the rawhide the Colville way: from the heel on up through the midsole and into the tip, like an offset spiderweb. Then he lacquered the rawhide. Last came the bindings, which his friend helped him with because the leather running strap was intricate in the way it crossed over the toe and around the boot; the harness itself was slit so the tightening girth could then be snubbed off.

Jake had fit his boots to the bindings three times that evening and had clattered about the cabin, trying to knock them loose on the stove, the door, the corner of the wood bin. But they wouldn't slip. He decided they were good to go.

Mallards waited. Prairie mallards always waited in Otter Bog. They fed and chattered about and seemed euphoric in their waiting, as if intuition told them that someday the bog might actually freeze and drive them off their aquatic riches. Then they'd have to try and dig into the fields, or move on. But Jake knew that the bog would stay open long after the nearby river and that the birds would keep gathering and festering, destined to the grassy bottoms that grew thicker each summer in this tucked-away gem in the middle of the high plateau. Jake could almost hear the muffled talk of the ducks in the early-morning falling snow. He could sense their reluctance to leave.

The snow that fell outside when he took his dog for a bedtime stroll was cold and light: December snow, crisp in its blue, icy ambiance. It was different from the heavier stuff that would come later on, just as the fine, fleeting crimson light of December was a light all its own. Jake thought of how fluent his new snowshoes would make him as he floated along in the white and absolute silence of the bogs, Colville style. He struggled to sleep, thinking of the morning filling with birds.

When he awoke, well before daylight, the snow had quit. He hustled some coffee, eggs, and bacon; fed his Lab; grabbed his coat, gun, and new snowshoes; and headed for the truck. Soon his pickup was humming through the foot of light snow, and he made good time over the county road that, aside from the river, was the only disturbance in a line of hayfields.

As Jake swung off the road and up the drive to the machine shed, his Lab came to life. Jake's foot trail from two storms before was barely evident. The wind had packed snow into it, and he decided to snowshoe beside it instead of on top, and he sank into the snow no more than a foot. The new shoes felt free and easy, and the motion soothed him by bringing him back to boyhood days when he'd run a small trapline in the thick woods of Michigan. The dog quickly figured out how to follow Jake's trail across the open darkness.

There were too many things to like about Otter Bog for Jake to have a favorite. As he shoed across the fields, working deeper toward the maze of alders bordering the ponds, he anticipated all of them. He loved the first tints of a slow dawn and the sounds of early wings. And he loved being in the bog alone, locked tight in the secrecy of it. He'd hunted in days of falling snow when every bird appeared low and silent and was shot within twenty yards. He'd hunted other mornings that were still and cold, when the hoarfrost clung thick as vanilla frosting to the alders—the whole bog one big, breathing, moving spirit, puffing jewels from its center. The dog's coat would turn to diamonds as soon as he exited the water, and Jake would have to put birds down as fast as he could to keep the dog in the water and keep him warm.

Jake hunted Otter Bog at least once a week, but never more than twice. The other mornings, he thought about it. By resting the spot in this fashion, Jake preserved the goodies and guaranteed himself an honest shoot. Now, with his new snowshoes, he would hunt it deep into the drifts of January and the season's end.

The white-tailed deer whose path he'd begun following after the first storms were using his old trail now. The snowshoe tracks would make it easier for them, too, and he'd make sure to clomp around in the thickets that the deer liked so as to help them out. Jake had crossed a cougar's track after the first storm but hadn't seen it since and had figured that the big cat would make its rounds and be back someday. He worried a bit for the deer, but he also appreciated the idea of the cat's using this hideout.

Jake reached the upper end of the bog first, where a pair of small ponds sat beside one another. He followed the outflow of the creek through the alders, down to the largest pond. Here he had a handful of decoys stashed under a tall pine, where a rack-laden buck often rubbed. Jake dug out the sack and threw the decoys beyond the rim of ice and into some grass. He took his snowshoes off and dug out a spot between two alder clumps. Then he pulled a few branches around himself and the dog, loaded his side-by-side, and settled down onto his pack, which he had placed on top of the snowshoes.

As night slowly dissipated into a growing gray dawn, he heard the first chatter. Jake chuckled on his call, and the dog tensed. Then he saw the dark silhouettes of birds above, as they stopped their wings and dropped like twisting missiles to the water between him and the decoys. Then the throaty quacks of confidence began, and soon the mallards were feeding amid the grass.

Jake slipped into consideration of other things. A heavy brook trout rolled beyond the ducks. A thrush stirred on an overhead branch. He sensed the buck stepping from behind the pine, and when he craned his neck to see, he looked straight into the deer's inquisitive eyes. When Jake turned back around, something tall and eerie moved from a place in the pond he'd been staring at all along: a blue heron began wading out from the seeping mist on its stilty legs, and at once Jake recognized the bird for the true apparition it was.

The ducks eased on past the decoys and moved slightly beyond gun range, but Jake heard more wings and he strained to pick out green heads as the birds splashed in next to him. He still couldn't distinguish the drakes, so he continued to wait.

Then the otter pack began its patrol: strong and shiny, four in all, they cruised straight for the decoys. Jake no longer feared they'd tangle in the anchor lines as he'd learned their navigational skills were from a different world altogether. They never ruffled the ducks, either, though his Lab watched them with unsettled curiosity.

Random snowflakes drifted groundward in seesaw fashion. In the next bunch of birds to come, Jake made out green heads. With slight reluctance he stood, swung through the leader, and broke the morning's calm with a pair of booms that left one drake upside down in the decoys. He quickly reloaded and tripped another drake that had gotten up from the far end of the pond. By the time the Lab was back with both birds, more circled.

Jake missed twice at a group of five, and he marveled at how lethal he was one moment, only to be so harmless the next. This is one thing that kept him fascinated with wingshooting: there were no absolutes—only that you wouldn't shoot perfectly for long. Ever. If you did the thing often, if you put yourself on the hunt at least a couple of times a week, you learned never to take a "good shoot" for granted. Jake had heard people say that ducks were easy—but from no one who'd spent any time at it.

Minutes passed, then a lone hen flew in. Jake let her settle, and soon a drake followed. He drew on the greenhead as it flared when he stood, and he missed clean with the right barrel. Then he got all of it with the left when the duck climbed straight away. As the dog made its way to the bird, three drakes came from the far end of the bog and began to land. Jake stood and doubled. Now, with just one bird left for a full limit, he debated whether to take it here or on his way out, jump shooting at the other ponds. He had ten minutes to debate before a pair of mallards started in; he swung on the drake and missed twice. A single greenhead came in minutes later, and he missed twice again. In amazement, he began to study the five winter-fat drakes at his feet.

Barely an hour had passed, but the early birds had slowed their coming. Jake knew he could sit and shoot ducks all morning if the law allowed, but the dog was starting to shiver steadily, and he opted to try his new shoes for sneaking and to pick up his last bird on the sly. He sent the dog after the decoys and then sacked and stashed them under the pine. He snubbed the mallards on a piece of baling twine, put his pack on, then hoisted the ducks over it. Cradling his gun, Jake began retracing his webbed path as the snow started falling in earnest again.

He wove his way along the creek's edge, stopping and studying each small puddle of water for any movement within. A lone hen startled him as she jumped from damn near under his feet. Jake cursed himself for not being more aware, and he stopped to gather in the aura of the snow—the solitude of the bog. Then he tried to move on within the boundaries of that silence.

At the northerly ponds, he saw ripples just beyond the cattails. He steadied the dog behind him and eased ahead on his shoes, picking his way among the cattail clumps. The anticipation began pounding in his head as he closed the distance to thirty yards, as he'd done a thousand times. This was another addictive symptom of wingshooting. Jake wondered which he liked more: a decoyed group of birds and the chance to pick and choose, or a perfect sneak to within solid range of an unsuspecting group of butt-up ducks. He knew all along that when the jump was made, no matter how prepared he thought he was, he would be swinging and shooting and praying strictly on instinct, as it all blew up in his face.

The pounding grew deafening as he paused to collect himself and make the jump. He could see three green heads. He savored the moment for as long as he dared, then stood. The ducks froze on the water, then burst up and reached hard for the far alders. Jake did remember to wait for them to line out, and just as they cleared the alder tops he swung on the crossing leader, drove the barrels through its head, and pulled. As if frozen, the bird fell into the bushes and the dog was after it.

Jake studied the fine plumage of the duck when the Lab delivered it. Winter mallards were not like any other of the year; their full-blown color was damn near fake in its brilliance. He treasured them, as he did Otter Bog: a place where raw imagery could be refined to the point of exactly that—animation. Be it the slow wag of a settling drake's tail or the dawn's transitory veil as it whispered the sound, *Shhh.*

Woodcock Vigil

Deep in the tangled creek is where we found them, with the honest-to-goodness November cold pressing down from Quebec. They were flight birds: in the last of the season on a blustery day when we had, until then, just two grouse to show for our efforts. And this was the year's final tour up north near the border with the one dog that had seen us from high school through college.

Earlier that day, along the great river that once was the main log run for much of this country, we'd been tempted to switch gears when a couple of flocks of black ducks hit a reed-choked eddy with reckless abandon they're seldom faulted with. The steel, cutting wind drove them.

We'd even limited our bush bashing to a pair of one-hour stints, with a warm truck drive in between. The two grouse had come close together early on and as much by accident as anything. But the righteousness of the day kept pulling us along because we hated to admit the woodcock might be gone and to be left only with deer season, a few ducks, and possibly some late grouse if we didn't get snowed out. None were my dog's favorite. Nor perhaps ours.

When I decided to head up to the base of the Notch, it was as much for sight-seeing as to check this covert I'd only been in once last December to shoot a grouse and get a Christmas tree. Lester was game for anything. And we swore to use the whole day. We parked, grabbed our gear, let the dog out, and started along what was left of an old skid road leading to the stream.

We hadn't gone far when the Brittany's bell went silent. Then a bird—the first woodcock of the day—came bursting out from the

27

roadside, which was thatched with alder, chokecherry, popple, and fir, and it headed straight away. Four shots only accelerated its escape, and as we stood with open guns, its mate flushed and fled down the same path.

Despite the cold, we weren't long "coming to," as what we were into after tracking frozen chalk for a few yards became obvious. The bell stopped once more, in cover that a month before was thick as an English hedge. But now I could see the dog and moved to come in from her port side. The bird rocketed up to the bare tops and I tracked it fleetingly all the way, only to miss with both barrels again. Lester missed once. My dog, who'd gotten quite adequate at the game, appeared nonplussed by all this and after that sort of glance, forged on along the stream.

The water cascaded down from the crest of an unnamed notch in the mountains whose sharp ledge walls had now gone to ice. The Granite State got named for these kinds of ledges, and the stream was tight and gnarled as the country it split. There is little doubt that it was a brookie haven, and a true nightmare to fish. But now that it was late bird season, the foliage all shriveled and fallen, we were able to pick our way toward the distant gravel pit where, after crossing the stream, the road led. Moose tracks still sucked moisture in the muck.

The next bird was all Lester's and after he missed it clean, we agreed to rest a minute, have a cigarette, regroup, and not waste this sudden and fading opportunity. After our smoke I left the lighter with the nice leather casing—a gift from my girlfriend—right there in the sweet-smelling, rotten fern next to that very stream that had all the right ingredients for woodcock.

The brief reprieve helped Lester, and he toppled the first of the next pair of birds to flush. And of the scores of woodcock taken before and after, that one particular alder-top-reaching brown ball, which suddenly folded at the report, remains framed in my mind as one of the finest and fanciest shots I can recall. Because it broke the ice on a day we couldn't have needed it more. For Lester, that is.

For me it was a different story. When I come out of a good shooting streak, I like to come out hard. One would think the last hunt of the season would be when you were at your best, having spent two months honing your reflexes on the "real thing." Yet we all know if we play the game long enough, dates have little relevance as to one's particular abilities during a certain day afield. I blame the stars, sun, moon, and what I had to eat or drink prior to a given hunt as much as anything. Still, it remains a plain mystery how one can so easily slump at the plate. It's a mystery like autumn geese. Perhaps the very mystery that keeps us coming back.

I used to keep track back when numbers mattered, which of course they do at some point, usually early on. I'd gone eleven for thirteen; killed eight straight; shot one hundred birds in a season, and so on. Just two weeks earlier that year, Lester and I had bagged two eight-bird Quebec limits with what couldn't have been more than a box of shells.

Enter one of the staunchest, most stubborn points I've ever seen my Brittany make. It happened right on the edge of a big frozen puddle in a maple grove some seventy-five yards from the stream. This was a forest floor, not a bird covert! Yet long ago I'd learned never to doubt the dog. I came upon my Brittany sideways, and a foot ahead of her twitching nose, from the mud and leaves, burst a russet rocket that made the fifty-yard line in a zigzag pattern that left my two loads of defensive No. 8s punching holes in the tree limbs. I broke the gun and barely reloaded in time for the second bird, which drafted its partner. I'll be darned if my shot pattern didn't do the same thing! If I wasn't beginning to feel frazzled, I at least was tingling with helplessness.

Still, my dog hadn't moved. I reloaded—out of habit more than anticipation, as I seldom if ever recalled flushing more than one pair of woodcock together. I even caught myself searching the bare ground in front of the dog, foolishly thinking just maybe I could see

29

. . . as if I did spot a sitting bird this would help me hit it when it flushed. I took a couple of slow steps closer, and bird number three corkscrewed up and out the back. I spun, I fired, and two more loads from my 28-gauge sped this bird on its way. Despite the daylong frost, my barrels were beginning to warm.

"You all right over there?" Lester hollered.

"You aren't gonna believe this."

"Need help finding birds?"

"You just aren't gonna . . ."

Woodcock number four almost joined his buddies, but my Brittany saw a wing go bad or something on my eighth shot and was off and running.

"I'll be goddamned!"

Lester got the cripple that wasn't so crippled when it sailed by him, out-shooting me a million to one for the first and perhaps last time.

The muck around that puddle next to that rambling stream must have been the last piece of unfrozen ground in northern New England. I'm not at all sure there weren't more woodcock right there in that hole, but my dog decided to go hunt with Lester after my despicable performance. She was likely hoping for the warmth of the truck heater and suspected that if we waited around for me to shoot my three-bird limit that day, we'd have needed snowshoes. It was as if I'd never before experienced the difference between the "locals" and the hard-driving flight birds with an agenda to get their butts down to Dixie.

In the end, I believe we counted seventeen separate flushes. Maybe I did finally shoot three birds, but I know it cost me a box of No. 8s and Lester may have helped. Walking out, I was elated and exasperated and full of chatter and "can you believes." All had gone down in an hour's time tucked up against those rugged New England hills a long, long way from where I etch these words. And then gone was gone: the birds, the season, the dog . . . that whole life.

Sometimes when the November air is just right though, as it is today, with the keen, cool smell of coming winter mixed with the ripe, soft, leftover fragrance of summer, I get lost on that day with Lester gunning "the flights" over Sadie. Say what you will, but never has my respect for the wonderful little woodcock been reinforced to such degree. And never have I seen someone demonstrate better how to make a three-bird limit last.

Desert Jewels

Winter . . . deep in Apache country
Dawn sounds like no other:
Cactus wren, Western bluebird
Phainopepla, Gambel's quail.
It is the Gambel's for which I wait—
Buried deep in the frost-covered sleeping bag
Not wanting to disrupt this peace of place.

Nearby, tight, even-tempered pointers
Dig deeper in their kennels
In an effort to ward off early-hour chill
Until they realize I'm awake
Then come begging to crawl up
So forgetful of their hard-earned toughness.
A late owl (I hope an owl) hoots in the distance
As the night log on the fire shifts.

When the fat moon fades
With the gathering, brilliant sun
I unzip and dump chunks of mesquite
Over the everlasting nighttime coals
And set the coffee to boil.
Charlie wakes to this;
The dogs crowd him while he lies silent
Probably thinking the same as I:
Three days left to the wild quail season
And we are in love with every moment.

It's so much more than filling limits now
The coveys are worn, and care must be taken.
You savor the big-hearted Elhews
Crossing out of creosote and yucca in streaks
To slam up hard in the grass-choked wash
With a Saguaro-dotted skyline
Cut by haunted purple canyons
Deep enough to hide refugees, indeed.

We marvel at just how tight
A dog's nose can get to quail
Without a flush. Then
At the speed with which they rise
Leaving your shot string behind one time
To be so surely tripped by another
A puff of feather and smoke left on the breeze.

Marvel at the soft bird in hand:
A smooth, airy impression
At sudden odds with this parched country
Yet so at perfect ease.
And talk the good talk
About all sorts of outdoor things
With an old, sturdy friend who knows
The desert, the quail, his dogs,
And sacredness.

Respecting each bumpy mile
Measured in boot-leather at the evening fire
Drawing birds after all the dogs are fed
Watered and sprawled around
At twilight when the border-splitting mountain range
Becomes an Indian lying down.

To sleep the good sleep
Under starry western skies
Dreaming to forever hear
The sweetest sounds of desert morn
Mixed with the first rustlings
Of strong-assed pointers galore
In some southwest quail camp.

A Sandwich for Ceremony

The sandwich began with most of a leftover grilled mallard breast. Then came sliced dill pickle, garden sweet onion, sharp cheddar, stone-ground mustard, a radish-alfalfa sprout mix, lettuce, and just a smidgen of plum jelly—all stacked between two thick slabs of dark Russian rye. It was a sandwich built, like Paul's Lab, for late-season ducking. Built the night before. Late the night before.

Paul had fought the drowsiness, waiting for lifelong pal Russ to arrive. His flight from Chicago put him in Spokane at 7:00 P.M., a three-hour drive from Paul's place. As the stove timer ticked toward 11:00, he speculated that he was doing well and that the last minute reunion—a sudden bachelor party as it were—was about to happen. But when Russ called at midnight and said, "Paul, I'm in *Seattle*," he knew their plans must take a desperate turn.

At best, Paul's house was a five-hour winter's drive from the city, on the other side of the Cascades. However, Seattle was but a four-hour jaunt from the spot he and his friend planned to gun on the Columbia River. Since Russ had just three days to hunt, missing a morning wasn't an attractive option. Paul's new idea: meet at the refuge before daybreak. Russ, only Russ, would pull an all-nighter. And Paul would easily have everything ready.

He overslept by a good half-hour and, as always, felt worse for a scattered four hours of sleep than for none. In haste, Paul made extra coffee, grabbed his pack, loaded the dog and himself into the Subaru, and headed down out of the mountains into a thick, January fog. Despite having to dodge numerous road-bound deer, Paul arrived at the refuge ahead of his man.

He wanted to hunt the barley field a couple of hundred yards from the river but was too tardy to get it on a Saturday—especially this late in the season, when the birds fed throughout the day and every "serious fowler" was out hunting. Instead Paul packed the canoe, three sacks of dekes, and a couple of gear buckets down to the waters' edge. He had a small blind on an island not far offshore and was about to shove off when Russ appeared. He'd had a hell of a midnight sojourn, but the symphony of geese, the whistle of widgeon, the raspy rustlings of early mallards, and the day coming fast automatically shot up the two friends with the right juice. They loaded Russ's stuff into the boat and embarked with little conversation. Soon daylight strained through the fog and they were set.

Any hunt that starts with no shooting at first light tends to make one queasy. There was shooting all right, but not for Paul and Russ. The barley field became quite active; they saw a couple of big shapes fall from the soupy sky when the first flock of geese hovered there and guns boomed. Another half-hour passed and all birds remained too far out and unwilling to examine their modest spread of decoys. During this final week of the season, the birds were as wise as they'd ever be.

Finally, as the two hunters began to lapse into conversation, a lone greenhead circled the outside of the spread. Paul gave a little feeding chatter, to which the duck settled.

"Yours, Russ. All yours."

Russ rubbed his eyes, quietly cleared his throat, looked at Paul, grinned, and stood to flush the duck. He missed cleanly with both barrels as the bird headed straight away.

"Jet lag," said Paul. "No biggie."

Russ grinned again. What hurt was that the next few birds couldn't be talked in. Another half-hour passed. More geese died in the barley. Then a lone honker from across the river headed toward them. It was low and noisy, and chances looked good. Paul tooted on the call as much as he dared, a breeze caught one of the floaters about right, and he was going to call the shot for Russ when another barrage from the barley flared the single goose and sent it on up river. Paul gritted his teeth.

"Ain't our fault, buddy."

"Nope. There'll be more."

But there weren't for a while, till a pair of suspicious widgeon came over the dekes on Paul's side. He held fire, thinking they'd circle and present Russ with a chance. Paul never saw them again.

"Shoulda' taken them," Russ said.

"Yeah. I was hoping . . ."

"Don't worry about me. I'm happier than I can tell ya just to be here."

Again, that filthy grin of Russ's.

"By God I'm some glad to have ya," Paul said, clapping his friend on the shoulder. "So, when did you say you were gettin' hitched? Man, I can't believe it. I mean . . . I figured if anyone were to outlast me it'd definitely be you. Now what am I gonna do? And I haven't even met her yet."

"I know. Who woulda thought? Thing is, she loves me. I mean, she really loves me."

"What the hell's she see in you? She just hasn't lived with you long enough. Obviously. She'll learn."

"That's what I'm afraid of. So we figured the sooner the better. May as well get on with it. First week in April."

"Where?"

"Chicago."

"Naturally. Couldn't have it anyplace nice."

"Well, it's her deal."

"Naturally."

"I don't want much to do with it. We both want it low key, but once her mother gets ahold of it . . . you know."

"Sorta'. Oops. Keep low. Can at nine o'clock. He's looking. Big bull. When he swings again, better take him."

At thirty yards, with the canvasback setting in, Russ pulled a repeat.

"Jesus, man. If just the thought of getting married messes your head this bad, I can't imagine your shooting after."

Once more Paul saw that familiar grin.

"Sorry you came all this way and not many birds, but you've had—"

"Hey. I don't care. We're here. That's what counts."

"Pretty special gal, huh?"

"Darlene is a good person. Definitely holds her own. No telling her what to do."

"Good."

More barley birds.

"Hey, we shoulda' hunted that field over there."

"No joke, Sherlock. What gives you that idea?"

"Well—"

"I didn't get here in time."

"You didn't *what*?"

"I slept in."

"Slept *in*! I drove all friggin' night and you—"

"Hey, chill. I thought you didn't care."

"Ha, ha. Oh, man. We've done all right haven't we? Been holding our own all along, by Jesus. Somehow, we manage to keep it going."

"Somehow."

"Not as much as we'd sometimes like, but we've been hunting a long time together for guys just thirty. Over half our lives."

"Yep. You've been making a great effort these past Thanksgivings. Both you and Jim. A damn fine ritual we've started, especially now that we're all spread apart. So far from New England, too. A long ways from woodcock."

"I'm tellin' ya, whew-ee. This kinda' shit don't happen in our generation much. Christ, we're old geezers, and we aren't even old."

"I know. We thought we'd never make thirty. Here we be!"

"And we just had to do this. So I skip teaching for a day. Whoop-tee-do. The kids will survive."

"We did. Hey, it's your bachelor party. Isn't like you had a choice."

A sudden movement caught Paul's eye. "There. Quick. Kill that greenhead."

Russ didn't. After missing the bird, he stood and stretched and hopped from one foot to the other, shivering.

"Gettin' a little white and wimpy livin' in the city, I see."

"I know it," Russ said. "Can't even take it when it's all the way up to ten degrees. Not even windy. Good thing for ole Johnson wool."

"Damn good thing. Saved us many a time."

"Truth to tell. Hey, you bring anything to eat? I think a little chow would bring me right into it. Nothing but airplane food for the last twelve hours and—"

"Did I bring anything to eat? What the hell you think this is, a second-rate operation? I've got something you might—" then a flash raced through Paul's mind, that he might have left the sandwiches on the kitchen counter. Frantically, he dug into his rucksack. His Lab, bored as a decoy by now, came right to life when Paul finally hauled a sandwich up from the bottom.

"Here," he said.

"What you got there!"

"I gotcha' breakfast. See what ya think of it, brotha."

"Mmmm."

As Russ started unfolding the paper sack, a gadwall drifted over-head.

"Bird!" Paul said.

"Take it," Russ muffled, trying to fit his mouth around the sand-wich. Paul stood and missed a straight overhead shot, as usual. The dog whined, but there came no rhetoric from his partner, as Russ finally ripped a bite from the mountain of real food.

41

Paul sat studying the way a breeze was stirring across the river and how a couple of bunches of ducks got up. A group of mallards headed into the barley, and more than one never left as guns thumped. Then Paul began to hear moans and groans of the type Paul figured only Russ's fiancée probably heard. Paul glanced at him. His friend's face was plugged. Suddenly, Paul thought he might be choking. But these were far from choking sounds. Gulping, perhaps.

"You gonna make it?"

"Mmmm—hmm—oh."

"Jesus, man!"

Finally, Russ got a swallow in and caught enough breath to say, "That is one *hell* of a sandwich," before he went for another bite, and continued cooing and eating.

Some birds were moving out now. A flock of redheads bore down on the island and when they split, the closest group was close enough. Paul folded one duck on the edge of the decoys, and finally the dog had something to do besides drool over scrumptious possibilities.

"Nice one," Russ muffled. He wouldn't even give the dog a bite of the sandwich when the Lab came back to the blind.

"Better eat fast. Birds are starting to move."

"No way. Can't. Too fine a sandwich. Worth the trip right there. Just what the doctor ordered."

By the time Russ finished eating, Paul had a widgeon, too, and had missed more redheads.

"You done yet?"

"Christ almighty, that's gotta be the second best sandwich I ever ate."

"And the first?"

"Can't remember. But there had to have been one. To be safe, I'll say the second best. My word, you take good care of me, Paul. Always have. We've never fallen short in the eating department."

"Enjoy it while you can. Sounds like you're gonna have a new caretaker. And you always wondered who was gonna take care of us when we got old."

"She could never make a sandwich like that. And I'm feeling myself come right into it."

"Good. See those mallards? They just got up from below the barley and are heading out this way. They've already been shot at in there, and they're getting blown offshore a little by the breeze. Here they come."

Russ cleared his throat, spit, smoothed the twin barrels of his old Stevens, belched satisfactorily, and hunkered low. Paul's calling got the birds to swing twice and start in to his side of the spread. He crushed a big drake, then held fire. "There we go. Bonus bird number one," Paul said.

When the dog brought back the greenhead, Russ's grin got bigger. "A beauty, too. Just as right as rain." He clapped Paul on the shoulder, this time.

Next, more redheads honed in on the decoys. Some say teal fly the fastest, but a redhead with a building breeze on its tail feathers moves right along. Any bird flying straight at the blind was a nightmare shot for Paul. He missed twice and didn't shoot his third shell. Russ center-punched the leader, which was traveling so fast that the dog had to run to the far end of the island to make the retrieve.

Then the geese came, bypassing the barley completely. They'd obviously already eaten and were looking for a place to rest and grind gravel. The island, they felt, was that kind of place. As they dropped without hesitation, landing gear stretching toward the water, they found how very wrong they were. Russ doubled; Paul managed one bird. And as the breeze turned into a wind, Paul figured he ought to try some sandwich—maybe to change his luck, as it had Russ's. Paul gave some meat to the dog and the last few bites to Russ. Minutes later, a bunch of handsome widgeon came into the decoys. Four went belly-up.

"Now we're cookin'," Paul said.

"Yes we are!"

Paul's reservations about Russ's losing a little enthusiasm for the hunt were erased.

A lull in both wind and birds came, and the conversation between the two old friends resumed.

"So. I don't suppose you want to come, do you," Russ stated more than asked. "I mean, I totally understand."

"Do you want me to?" Paul understood Russ's way of using reverse psychology, having known him since kindergarten.

"Sure. It'd be great if you and Jim and some of the guys came. But I understand."

"Screw you, Russ. Of course I'll come. It's a landmark event."

"Well . . ."

"Well nothing. Don't be an ass."

In the silence that followed, Paul drifted back. The fishing and the hunting and the skiing stood out. Mostly, the fishing and hunting: the lush, high-mountain streams for fat July brookies, the flaming red and orange October woods for grouse and woodcock. The sweet hard-working, big-hearted dogs; the worn-out leather; the boot-burning campfires; and the bottles of cheap whiskey, now all gone. Because Paul fished and hunted mostly alone, he was reluctant to "let go" of one of the few people who shared a similar philosophy and appreciation of these matters. That philosophy came from their common home ground and families. And it was one they had carried everywhere with them.

Since moving to the city, an act unheard-of ten years prior, Russ seemed to be saying more and more that they really hadn't changed and wouldn't change—as if trying to convince himself. But he'd already changed. And marriage, from what Paul had seen and heard, was a substantial change. So Paul supposed he had reason to feel a smack of melancholy—that he was not only losing a part of Russ, but that perhaps he was the one, for once, staying behind. Usually they took equal turns in the stern when it came to running uncharted waters. This time, they paddled separate boats.

The next hour refocused Paul on the immediate. There came another barrage of in-your-face birds, and the two friends were swinging and shooting and taking the remainder of their ducks in the form of mallards and canvasbacks. Paul had seldom seen Russ shoot so well, particularly since he'd come straight from a midwinter, inner-city classroom where he'd conjured a new kind of toughness all foreign to Paul.

They waited into the afternoon in hopes of more geese. Perhaps the same loner that had been scared off in the morning was the one that came back: a large, beautiful honker that seemed a good one to call it quits on. Russ shot him cold at twenty-five yards and at once the two men realized that they'd had a fine-enough day. He and Paul decided a good night's sleep would ensure a promising tomorrow. Plus, Paul had a stash of good bourbon that demanded their attention. After all, it was Russ's bachelor party. Someone had to give it. Just he, the dog, himself, and three gray days of late-season gunning.

By the time they had the decoys picked up, the wind had laid down so as to afford them a good crossing in a canoe full of birds and guns and more memories to take along the flow of time. They left Russ's rental car, stuffed Paul's vehicle full, and headed for a coffee stop, then into the mountains with thoughts of slow-barbecued goose breast and lots of easy conversation on their minds. And a great hope of Paul's: that good gunnin' and good eatin' would always keep the common link between them well oiled. Always.

...

At the rehearsal dinner, in a very fancy place in downtown Chicago, Paul finally met Darlene—nearly as tall as six-foot-two-inch Russ. She seemed an attractive and sincere-enough gal. Paul told her that, come summer, they must visit him in the mountains, if for no other reason to pick up their wedding present, a signed print of spring swans he'd gotten at the annual DU banquet.

"Only if I get one of your sandwiches," she replied.

"Huh?"

"Oh God, that's all Russ could talk about when he got back from his bachelor party—the sandwich you gave him out on the river. He went on and on for days about it. Said it made the whole trip and is the only reason he survived the first day. Sounds like I've a lot to live up to."

"Yeah. But you gotta drive all night through snowy passes and foggy river bottoms and then sit in a cramped, wet duck blind first to truly get the gist of it. You've got to understand the full value of a good sandwich."

"So I hear. I'm willing."

"Well, I'll do my best to spare you the extremes."

"It's a deal."

"By the way," I said. "You have excellent taste."

"In sandwiches?"

"No, in men. They come no finer."

"Yeah, he's all right."

"However, when you get sick of him—which I guarantee you will—just send him out to me for a few days of shooting. I'll straighten him out and he'll return a new man. Deal?"

"Deal."

Georgia

Georgia stood solid, pointing grouse, when Tom raised his sleek double-barrel and blasted her in the head. Bird shot works on spaniels, too. At five feet it's quick as a vet's needle and just as sterile. The sterility is what bothered Tom to begin with. Besides, Georgia hated the vet's. And when all is done, dead is dead.

Grouse come hard in December in New Hampshire, especially during a raw morning drizzle. They feed early and late, and stay tucked in the rest of the time. The bird Georgia pointed may have known that today a different game was being played. It sat tight between a juniper bush and apple tree on a hillside where Georgia had learned some things about grouse—and man. The bird flushed at the shot; Georgia lay behind. She lies there still, looking west, firm in the stubborn New England turf.

Fourteen years is about all a dog can answer. Fourteen years and yesterday didn't seem much different to Tom. He imagined this might be what it's like to shoot yourself. Memories raced, running into one another with no discretion, blurred as the cooling mist blurs and softens the balsam fir. There was no way of keeping track.

Was it actually years ago . . . when Georgia and Jake's dog, Cleo, stood pointing the same woodcock in that great old orchard up north? Finally the two bitches came to agreement on something—a pair of dogs so identical in their ways that they were always at each other from the ride up early in the morning, till the end of the ride home at night. They would share the back seat out of necessity only, growling the entire time and making the car stink with that certain mix of woods and wet after a late October day in the north

47

woods. Tom could almost smell it: the sweetness of rotted ferns; mushy apples; dank, muddy feet.

He remembered saying then to his friend how unorthodox their two dogs truly were. But they were all dog and got the job done, and the two hunters would miss them awfully when each was gone. Today was the first day of Georgia being gone.

Hard days come for those who think daily about dying; Tom recalled Jake's words. Far as he knew, Georgia hadn't thought much about dying. If at all. Only the last couple of days and today, when she woke on her messed blanket, shaking. She'd barely had the strength to crawl under the couch, where she wouldn't come out because she was too proud to be seen as something she was not. Dignity. Dignity was something he would not let her lose. Tom felt thankful for this privilege.

He was thankful, too, for the time and place to take care of his own. He had brought Georgia to this hillside of their first hunts because he knew it was the only thing that would pump the life back into her, so he could take it away: drawing down on his closest friend, wanting to kill faster and cleaner and more unsuspectedly than he'd ever killed before as she stood etched like granite in the scraggly, brown pasture. Countless miles of bird cover were on her legs—a thousand points in her heart. The full moment of truth, is all; this was the best Tom knew how. Now the thin, mountain rain blended Georgia's blood with the rusted leaves.

After he lifted the dog by her limp legs—her head rolled back, her leather bell-collar chewed through by the shot, her smooth hair matted—he wrapped her tightly in the wool hunting coat he pulled from his back, carefully eased her down in the ground, and, using the shovel he'd brought, placed the last bit of stony dirt over her. Then he stood, rolled and lit a cigarette, and drew the smoke deep. He leaned heavily against the callused bark of the apple tree behind him.

Already, the shot sounded surreal to him—an echo from some

gone and away place—the tangy odor of gunpowder taken over by that of fresh tobacco.

He thought of the friends he'd have to tell the truth to. The telling, he figured, might be worse than the doing. Then he tried to think just of his friends. There was the hope of another dog someday, too, and more hunts to come. There would be other fine things in this life, he knew, but all that good was far away now.

Tom studied the thick, blue wood smoke moving hesitantly into wet air, and drifted with it. It brought him back again to the times and places he loved most. To where he felt the poignant October days that hung in the balance between summer and winter; the trade winds between green and white. Days that always seemed to come too slowly and disappear too fast; days looked forward to and looked back upon equally; days that were viscous . . . like the morning's waking hour. And never caught up with.

He felt the coolness and could see the bright colors of a new bird season. He tasted the sweet-cream sky. He watched as a dainty orange-and-white dog trotted back to him with a sideways gait on a dirt road deep in the north country, surrounded by a thickly wooded, rolling land much bigger than her small, invincible, rugged body. He saw her at the end of the day, with a grouse he doubted he'd ever touched jammed so tightly in her mouth that it pinched her eyes shut. The bird had been found only because she had learned to break at the shot, see a loose feather Tom couldn't, and mark falls through some transcendental pathway of her own. And he had let her be free here—free to follow rules not made by man.

Tom allowed himself to stay back in the years. The weight of them held him against the tree for a very long time, until the day had grown and some eternal clock inside that had yet to fail him tolled, and he recognized the time for leaving.

A chickadee sounded high in the treetops, then fluttered to a birch. Rain changed to snow, gray air to chalk. Soon Georgia would be tucked in the silence of winter's blanket, the whole thing made clean again, till spring, when the woodcock would come, dance and sing, and when the grouse would strut past her grave.

Tom said goodbye to Georgia. He picked up his shovel and shotgun, and started back along the stone wall leading to the broke-down barn and his truck beyond. Forcing his eyes from this place of no return. Forcing his eyes to focus on the earth turning white in front of him.

Mountain Blues

Different from the grouse of a week ago,
Their wings make me hasten
Flash my eyes, grip my gun.
The dog has them going on the rock outcropping
Steep as a horse's face, while the sun breaks the high ridge
And softens blueberries, juniper, ka-nic-a-nic.
Meadowgrass, heavy with sugar-thick frost
Loosens, wakens sleeping hoppers.

Gold-fringed larch illuminate snow-freckled peaks
For hawks to stretch against. Dawn light deepens,
Sprinkles the ice-rimmed lake with age-old jewels
And chases about cloth-scattered mist.
Late wildflowers bathe as I shed smoke-scented wool
     and slide on up.

This September world rising makes me glad of my own;
So fine to have left campfire comfort for
These sweet birds, these private pastures.
It is near enough that the dog has them going,
Near enough to hear fresh wings.

A blue shape bursts, hurtles overhead
Trailing nothing but sky, and all recollection is lost
All recollection is gained
In sudden, swinging movement.
In sudden feathery completion.

On the Plateau

Charlie didn't think much of the great wide-open spaces when he first drove west at age nineteen. They even scared him. Made him feel small.

He couldn't find familiar boundaries in the endless sky and the rolling land that was broken into grain. There weren't any of the trees, stone walls, streams, and fences that so defined his New England. His heart started to sink when he drove out of Saint Paul and hit the northern plains that stretched clear to the Rockies. And it sank all the way a couple of days later, when his nine-hundred-dollar pickup truck blew a head gasket climbing up from the Columbia River, just shy of Washington's wheat country. The eastern part of the state and its undulating expanse of treeless scab land, cut by a mighty river-turned-pond, had made him wonder if the Pacific Ocean wasn't just some made-up feature on a map in his freshman geography class.

Charlie smiled as he recalled this first impression of the prairie—all kinds of prairie country—fifteen years earlier, as he lay next to his Lab on the hard, cold December ground with only a faded Carhartt work suit and some wheat straw to hide him from the geese and insulate him from the wind. He'd now lived in the Northwest for more than a dozen years, and his love for open spaces had grown considerably, as had his lifelong love for waterfowl. The result: frequent trips to the Columbia plateau country, which increased his infatuation with both.

The emptiness that had once scared him now drew him in. That and the birds—those great, great birds down from some other prairie

53

still farther north—finally driven out because Canada had frozen as
stiff as the basalt outcroppings that broke up the rolling wheat.

The birds . . . Where the hell were they? As Charlie listened to
the wind whistle through the abandoned homestead that still stank
of pack-rat dung and marmot behind him, he wondered if Tim had
gotten the field right. "Up behind the house on Patterson Coulee," his
friend had phoned excitedly the night before. "Thick as ants for two
days now."

Charlie couldn't deny the fact that he was lying in pretty fresh
goose scat, but it had been two hours since daybreak, and the only
thing that had changed was the wind; it now gusted from the south,
twice as strongly as before. The air temperature hadn't caught up
with the southerly flow, so his feet and hands—as usual—were too
cold for him to take a nap for fear of losing them. He could have used
a nap, too, having awoken at three o'clock to make the ninety-minute
trip to meet Tim, driving another half-hour to the field, and spending
an hour setting out their modest eight dozen silhouettes and shells.
Charlie envied his Lab, who'd already fallen asleep against the
warmth of his leg. Fight as he might, Charlie was beginning to get that
destitute feeling he'd experienced when his adolescent truck blew
up in this foreign land long before. The difference was that he now
had several memorable plateau goose hunts, thanks in large part to
Tim. They kept him warm and prevented the huge leaden sky from
getting the best of him. At this temperature, a change to the south
meant just one thing: snow—always a hunter's friend.

"They'll be back," Tim mumbled from beneath his straw hutch,
some ten yards away. "You easterners are too damn pessimistic."

"Realists," Charlie retorted.

"Pessimists. The geese haven't been disturbed. They'll be back."

"Whatever. I'm just getting a little tired of the same view. Think
I'll get up and get some circulation going. Dog needs to pee."

"Hell, Charlie, that Lab's an eastern-Washington dog. He knows
all about patience and what to do while he's waiting for birds. Take

54

a nap why don'tcha. Wake up to my gunshots."

"Ha, ha. I would, but I'm afraid of frostbite."

"Frostbite! It's gotta be at least fifteen degrees out!"

"Exactly."

"Well, don't be too long. Get caught out fooling around, and we're both frigged."

"I know, I know."

"Hey, what was that?"

"Ravens, Tim. The only thing this country is fit for. Ravens and coyotes."

"Boo-hoo."

Charlie began to crawl from beneath his straw pile and was halfway to his knees when Tim whispered: "Down! Them ain't ravens, bud."

Charlie barely made out the sound of distant geese, so very faint and ghostlike at first. He scurried back under the straw and studied the horizon for the broken line that was sure to appear. There were no substitutes.

No substitutes and no feeling to catch your spirits like that unmistakable, multisyllabled, almost mournful language of towarding geese. Nothing like looking over the silhouettes and seeing that black line, the only mark in the sky.

The sound grew—still exciting and strange to Charlie. Yet no great line evolved. Then he could pick out movement above the far-thest basalt outcropping: a small bunch of birds headed low and right at them. Tim gave a few loud calls and then fell silent, as the geese couldn't be lined up any better.

There's nothing so empty as an open sky with no birds in it, and nothing so full as an empty sky with just one goose in it. Four were in the approaching group, and when they got some three hundred yards out they eased their pumping to a few solitary beats, set their wings, and—murmuring—glided on the heavy air, right for the hole in the decoys.

Their feet were fence-post high when Tim called the shot. Charlie remembered to concentrate on his two birds, focusing just on their heads. As fast as four trigger pulls, the sky was all feathers and the geese lay flat on the ground. Charlie's Lab went from a sound sleep to a full run and had the birds picked up in seconds. The plateau went still again.

"Four birds didn't make all these turds," Tim said. "But if they want to come in groups like that, it's okay by me."

Another half-hour passed and the great landscape didn't change, save for the fact that the wind found a few snowflakes somewhere and brought them in fits and starts to the goose hunters. Then came that sound again: isolated and glorious. This time it grew and grew until it seemed a thousand birds were jostling for position—as if the heavens were full of their tongue only.

There weren't a thousand but a solid hundred in the next flock to break the horizon. "Want to hunt tomorrow?" Tim asked

"Damn right."

"Then take your stretch now. Keep this group out of here."

"Ten-four." Charlie got up and walked out to the front of the decoys to take a leak. The big flock of geese gradually slipped side-ways as they approached and then passed the spread a few hundred yards to the east. Charlie returned to his straw grave.

"We'd've had 'em," Tim assured. "Too much left in the season for that, though. There'll be more."

There weren't for some time, and the snowflakes became more regular. The next time Charlie heard anything, it was Tim's snoring. He smirked and debated whether or not to wake his friend by calling, or just to wait and see if the geese would come on their own. He wished he'd brought his camera. He decided to keep quiet.

When Charlie could see the birds in the spitting snow, there were fewer than a dozen and they were slipping to the east. He started calling. The geese called back and hesitantly circled. This time they came in from behind the homestead. Charlie strained his eyes to the west and could see the Canadas pass over the weathered house, standing solid against the whitening sky. He closed his eyes and softened his calling. Tim hadn't joined him and Charlie wondered what the trouble was. He couldn't worry about his friend, yet these birds needed some serious convincing. He concentrated on his calls, mixing high and low notes, grunts, growls, and double-clucks—trying to imitate Tim's trying to imitate geese. The birds set up but hung about fifty yards out and then slipped again. They began to leave and Charlie started hailing. Once more the geese turned back.

Charlie wondered what in the world his partner was doing. This time the geese set in from the east and were a little lower. They came over the outside of the spread some forty yards out. Charlie didn't know what to do—whether to call the shot or just shoot or what. He never moved while the geese passed by, circled farther out, and sped off to the east.

"Dammit," Charlie spat aloud.

"You did the right thing," Tim said quietly from his mound. "No sense screwing up a chance at getting them all the way. Fifty-fifty they woulda committed on the next pass. Nice job, bud."

"You were awake! Why didn't you—"

"Was waitin' to see how far you'd come. Not bad, Chuck . . . for an easterner."

"You woulda—"

"Never know. What's this?"

Three geese appeared low over the wheat and set their wings. As they glided into the spread they looked as if they might overrun it, but in a flurry of backpedaling, they landed practically between Charlie and Tim.

"Go!"

Charlie killed the lead bird as they flushed, Tim shot the next one, and the third goose crumpled as they both fired.

"Yee-haw!" Tim hooted. "That's why we do it. That's why you

let the maybes go. What goes around comes around, Chuck ol' boy. Look at those birds. Big'uns."

Big they were; the Lab struggled to flip them up into his mouth. Their wings dragged as he brought them back to Charlie, who threw more straw over the pile of geese.

It was snowing in earnest now. Charlie's thoughts drifted with the flakes. As a boy he'd read about field-hunting geese on the Eastern Shore of the Chesapeake, and very occasionally about the same kind of shooting in the West. Both had always seemed a remote possibility at best. Now that the experience was reality— something he did on sort of a regular basis—the magic only intensified. The birds themselves, no matter how many he'd fooled to the dinner table, remained just as mysterious, wise, and splendid as ever. And he felt no more part of their world now than before; he simply shared more time with them, and felt fortunate to live where he could hunt them successfully. But he knew up here on the plateau was no place to get cocky. This country could eat you alive, with or without geese. With geese, the wild only became that much more intriguing.

"Want to wait it out?" Tim asked. "Maybe pluck our last one from a small flock?"

"Sure. For a little while. But let's not botch up tomorrow."

"I hear ya."

Ten minutes passed, and a flock of some thirty birds came out of the snow. They would have landed in the spread if Tim hadn't scared them off. Then another flock came. Then another. The harder the snow, the more geese.

It still baffled Charlie how wary these otherworldly creatures could be one moment, only to act so seemingly foolhardy the next. He shot them in his imagination a few times, then just watched them in grace as they circled and drifted in the swirling snow, typifying a most raw and elegant dance.

"How 'bout it Chuck? Just you, me, and the dog."

Charlie was silent. The Lab, his face all white with snow now, shook beside him under the straw.

"Hate to do it, but let's get outta here," Tim said after a spell.

"Roger that. We'll get that last bird tomorrow."

"You got that right."

After they had their spread collected, Tim got the truck and drove to the edge of the field. They packed in the geese and decoys, and Charlie told Tim he'd meet him at the intersection after giving his dog a walk.

As Charlie and the dog approached the old homestead, surrounded by mule-drawn field discs, a monolithic combine, and a rusted grain drill—a few curtain shards flapping crazily in the wind and the sound of geese building behind him—he tried to figure out if this strange juxtaposition of new agriculture and wild geese was a good one or not. It seemed fine, but he doubted the settlers of this sharp country ever witnessed birds in such numbers. Charlie knew the dire consequences of many modern agricultural practices; still, he couldn't wait till tomorrow. He would always be a foreigner in the plateau country. Then again, who wouldn't? Even the geese themselves, he felt, were mere visitors. Though oftentimes it seemed as if this place belonged to them, they would stay around as long as opportunity afforded it, then disappear . . . leaving behind only that fit for the wind.

Charlie and his Lab turned for the warmth of the pickup with thoughts of a new tomorrow already building inside.

Holding Ground

Nate studied the collar and bell through the steam of his afternoon coffee. He studied the box of 28-gauge No. 9s and the whistle, and knew the rest would pass too soon. The season was two-thirds over; his shotgun remained stuffed somewhere in the closet. But Nate knew the time for going was now. Now, he had to go. This was not the time for letting up, he thought, for the dog if for nothing else.

She's much brighter now, coming into her twelfth season. Brighter than the past couple of years, when she had to share Nate with a younger Brittany. The young male was now gone, crushed by the wheels of a pickup.

All the talk Nate had heard about a young dog keeping an old dog spry couldn't have proved more contrary. The day that all of Nate's ambitions came to a screaming stop on that untraveled, winter-frozen road was a day of lifted weight for the older dog. She never particularly liked the second dog to start with. It was that plain and simple. Dogs don't fake.

Nate labored to forgive her in her jubilance. He labored even though it made perfect sense, she having been the only one for so long. He'd been so careful with the younger dog, giving him things he hadn't known when the female was a pup. Things he learned largely from her. The patience finally paid off, too. In just two seasons, the young dog had become quick on woodcock, was becoming staunch on grouse, and was retrieving nicely on both land and water.

The whole thing made Nate want to hurl his coffee cup as hard as he could against the cast-iron woodstove, smashing it to fragments as the truck tires had splintered the young dog's back, leaving

Nate with the hollow knowledge it was his own fault only. The end so close to the beginning.

Now down to one dog again, Nate found the older Brittany staring at him. She shuffled across the hardwood floor to get closer, remaining sort of half-sitting while she did so. Subtle, but making herself plenty evident in her dainty fashion, the same way she begged. He reached down and felt her smooth, sleek head and her soft-coated back.

Having shared a variety of things their bond ran deep, and now they shared in this. Company for his lonely hours: humorous, aggravating, and quiet. And though not the most orthodox, a New Hampshire woodcock dog through and through. Now an old woodcock dog. She had in her what some dogs could never get. The populations of humans and birds were changing that fast.

Nate would head to the river this afternoon, the river that split the mountain valley in two. Clear, cold, gravel-bottomed, curving down from the highest mountains, it flowed southeast for a hundred miles to the ocean. A hundred miles of boulder-filled rapids and long, quiet pools. A hundred miles of the richest farmland in the Northeast. This was the river Nate grew up on, as had his dogs. Their learning grounds, about woodcock and ducks, mayflies and trout. About some differences between indoors and out. About the ecology of a healthy place, an uncrowded place.

Nate enjoyed the luxury of slowly driving the roughed-out farm road down through the fields. The same fields where he'd learned not to wear shorts while haying and how to stack bales just right on a flatbed. Little had changed here, except for the cluster of condominiums built at the beginning of the road. Built on the one piece of land here that farmers no longer owned. The only piece of land safe during a large flood.

The driving was a luxury compared to Nate's high-school days when he had to wade the river, crossing down by the family farm in order to then head north. Legs numbed by the piercing water, feet wet, socks and boots full of sand—but a fresh box of shells to burn.

The dog sat up in her seat as they eased down the road. She recognized it all. Felt this as different from any other side road. They hunted here only on occasion now, instead of every other day as they had when she was a pup. Nate looked over at her with her graying muzzle, her watering eyes and wondered where her time had gone.

Bird cover ran the whole length of the river north of the farm. However, these upper fields seemed more the middle of the covert. From here Nate had the option of hunting north and south, and he didn't have to worry about fording the main river. He could simply skip across the rapids in the middle of the still water and hunt either way.

There were enough big trees and fences and stream crossings to discourage most other folks from hunting here—or at least to hide the "real cover" from them. Nate knew of only a few who'd hunted these pieces of cover, and they did so by accident only, seldom ever to find their way back again.

Today he decided he would hunt across the still water, on ground he called the "small island," then cross the stream back to the south, onto the "big island." With the bird limit cut almost in half, they'd probably never get far, but this was the plan he and the dog discussed.

The Brittany leaped out of the truck before Nate could stop her. This used to bother him, but he could care less now. He slid her collar and bell into one vest pocket, and the box of No. 9s into the other. He unsheathed his double, looped the whistle that the dog couldn't hear anymore over his head, threw the keys on the floor, and closed the truck door.

The stink of it is what made Nate wish he could do things all over again—made him wish the dog were young. The stink of fallen dead leaves and of moist, cool, river-bottom soil. No breeze stirred. The day was clear, just beginning to turn gray. It smelled a little like snow. How had the seasons melted into November so fast?

How had the time from the days of high school to those of a searching man in a growing and confusing world passed so fast? The span, as it were, was no more than a good dog's lifetime. Torn between what he felt as the old and good, and the new and not so good, Nate followed his dog into cover same as always.

The flights would certainly be here now, he figured. It had already snowed a couple of times farther north. The dog hunted a bit fast at first, naturally excited. She passed over ground that both she and Nate were surprised held no birds. He wasn't sure if the dog had skipped them, or there flat-out were none. Long ago, he'd learned never to second-guess her. Still, the emptiness disturbed him, haunted him even.

In these golden years of hers, the dog knew the covert by heart. She knew where to go when one spot failed. She knew where not to waste time. The ground was drier than ever this year, and the birds knew this as well as anything. They would be along the moisture of the river—somewhere.

She hunted down through some scrub cherry and maple, then into the clump of birch before stopping cold under a stunted pine. The silence of her bell made the murmur of the slow river return to Nate's ears. All else was still. So quiet that Nate's own steps in the sand annoyed him. He, too, stopped.

Then he listened. Things all started coming back on him. But Nate was older now; he had experienced so much since the dog was young. He felt a blinding urge to fight back, to fight hard against what already had become distant memories and boyhood feelings. But there was more than he expected.

The severe presence of the sheer granite ledges behind the weathered barn downriver seemed to echo his thoughts. The ledges stood there as if a glacier had cut them straight off the side of the other mountains, similar to the way a cleaver might slice a piece of cheese.

Then there was the sugar orchard bordering the large field below the barn on one side, the river on the other. The orchard's thick-trunked maples saved much of the earth from being swept seaward along with their old, gnarled roots. Beyond, the rich hayfields lay pale with autumn.

Lavender mountains encompassed it all, their features more defined with the absence of leaves and an etching of snow. And the highest one was now broad and fully white, standing guardian-like straight upriver, its grand reflection unwavering in the quiet of Nate's first trout pool.

Nate was the sixth generation of his family who had stood here. He couldn't pretend any more than he could let up now.

Such a big valley, really, he thought. Big in the variety of land and onslaught of rugged weather. Big in things to do and what it held for memories. So very small, however, in its fragileness. He didn't like what some people had done to the valley, people who had a different idea, a different meaning of "the worth of the land." They would never know just how much this place was worth if left untouched. And even if they did, he just couldn't swallow the fact that he might have to make room for them to visit or live here, too.

Nate swallowed hard on his tobacco, opened the box of No. 9s, and dropped two into the worn barrels of the double. He walked along the edge of the covert until he came parallel with his dog. He spoke to her again, low and soft, and moved in through the brush toward the pine she was under.

He was five feet from her now. Suddenly, he saw the eyes of the brown bird, sitting in brown leaves, placed there carefully enough to be a fake. He saw the brown back of his dog, still stiff. And just as the pieces were blending together, just as brown turned gold and keenness built in Nate, the little bird broke the spell by disappearing into a whir of wings.

Nate followed it now, followed its twisting flight up against the lines of bare trees and out toward the river. He was all movement,

65

pushing the barrels at something he now traced by instinct. The bird grew small against the snow-covered mountain. Nate swung on and on until it felt okay, until he could see the bird clearly as a bird. Until it seemed good again.

Later, Nate sat by the edge of the slow-moving water cleaning birds. He watched as their autumn plumage drifted gently downstream. In pieces, they would float until they lodged on a snag or logjam, where they would make easy food for some other creature. Somehow going back into the health of the river. Still, he felt some remorse to leave them scattered so, for he adored these little birds. It felt somewhat odd that their epic journey south ended so soon this way. He only soothed himself by feeling that it seemed better here, rather than farther along—somehow. If anyone was to say at all.

He wished for woodcock always along this river. He knew it was their lifeline through the mountains, and generally a safe one. They had to come here. If they stopped coming here, they would stop coming altogether.

The moon was waxing again, into another month. The night air settled heavy into the river, and the orange glow on the snowfields of the mountain faded to pink, to purple. The dog's breath and Nate's breath mixed, hanging rich in the delicious, moist air.

Nate smiled as he looked at the Brittany, grooming herself clean beside him in the riverbank mud. He was glad she could be part of this world. Glad that her life had been a healthy one and, most of all, that they had shared in this.

The river grew loud, the rush of the rapids below coming at once alive. The forever changing flow that mineralized the soil each spring but also decided for itself just how much of a hay field a farmer was allowed to keep. Or how many sugar trees or what kind of fishing holes or where one might hunt. It also decided what man could or could not destroy.

Nate listened to this perpetuator of life. He listened to the river's rocking wave, its pulsing course, the heartbeat of this ancient mountain and timeworn valley. And he felt right about what he and the dog had done that day. As he drifted back over different years of woodcocking, a pair of birds whistled in overhead to settle for the night, their long beaks making strange silhouettes in the shine of water and moon. Nate decided it was a time and place never to lose touch with. He decided, all and all, that it probably couldn't get any better.

For the Keeping

My boot slides around the bottle
Hidden as if a smooth, round rock.
Too hard for breaking, browner still
Than the flood of hardwood leaves
Falling like snowflakes
In the gusting north wind.

The dog nosed it first.
Her bell stopped not quite long enough
For grouse. Quiet enough
To draw me off the course I weave
Through tight, small trees.

Short necked, fat bottomed
It's the kind for cleaning,
For filling again and for capping
Something good,
Something needing to be kept well.
Long enough to seal
And age a good thing.
Thinking of worn-down mountains:
They are aged and plenty good.
No . . . not that long.

Thirsty now, I must drink
From the cool mountain brook
Then wash the sludge
From this quart-sized find.
Clean and fresh again,
I slip it into my vest pocket
Where I'd morning long
Hoped to put a fat grouse.

We rest between a muffled stream and
The concave, vacant nest in leaves
That by day's end will be full again
With more assorted copper caps
From trees the same color as the dog.

She is old enough to be good;
Now she knows about grouse.
She thinks there's a bird ahead;
I think the wind too strong
For much of a hunt today. Except, perhaps,
Relics in the wood.

But she is over the wall and gone again
With the deftness of a dog half her age.
I am off following
Through this lazy autumn dream,
A similar weight of grouse
Sagging my pouch.

Good find, girl.
I'll take it home:
Boil it, clean it inside out
Then fill it with the thickest winter stout.
And keep this bottle on a shelf
Remembering, glass by glass—
All that time.
Long after
You are gone.

Alas . . . only mortal creatures here.

A Hunter Looks at Forty

About the time Holt felt the long withdrawal coming on, the lazy Indian-summer weather of the past week took a turn south. With November pressing down, the prairie, which now shared itself heavily with grain, was shot with gold as the lengthening shadows built in the coulees and on the round rolls of plateau.

Chewed-on clouds stalled overhead in an effort to give the sky some sort of definition in its luminous, if not ominous, expanse, which was cut short only by the Cascade mountain range some hundred miles to the west. There wasn't much farming to be had now with the harvest and fall planting behind him; Holt knew the time for walking had come. He felt boyhood urges swell up in the form of crisp days and open country with nothing but dogs and birds and a building silence that may well have been the coming winter's ghost.

He sat alone most of the evening on the porch, since Becky— now seven months pregnant—was gone to Spokane to be with her mother for a few days. He felt the change of seasons coming while he thought about grain prices, the government, corporate farms, that girl Karla, and finally his shorthaired pointers, which paced back and forth as if they were on a fifteen-minute timer keeping track of the hours. Holt had found his bear grease and hunting boots and had gotten to palming them, recognizing that they still needed new soles and wondering if they'd be worth anything in the rocks. He knew the dogs would be a mite tender the first couple days, so he would have to stay clear of the steepest slopes of shale and concentrate instead on the brush-choked draws, the edges of the wheat, and the tall

native grasslands and sage that his father had made a habit of keeping through all the years he had built up the ranch.

His father's words came back to him just then: "Same thing that
makes you live can kill you in the end." As the ranch surely had his
father, though it took seventy years. All things told, that suddenly
seemed like a long time. Truth to tell, Holt himself was getting to feel
that seven decades might be a bit too long. Right then he was glad to
have sold all the spring and fall grains straight out of the field. "No sit-
tin' and waitin'—just sold and thank you Christly little," as his
neighbor Clyde used to say.

All summer long he had waited for now. All through the spring
cultivating and planting, the summer harvest, and finally the late-
August taking of his hard spring wheat. Then the fall planting. Now
he could head out and let the land he and his father worked so hard
to hold onto rustle his body and soul. Holt had kept his dogs in
decent shape simply by letting them follow him along while he was
farming. Since he had cut out herbicides—chemicals altogether, after
his father died—not only were the birds staging a resurgence, but the
dogs could run about at will. They were deer-broke and snake-broke
and didn't pay coyotes a whole lot of mind, so the three of them had
little to hurt or get hurt by out here on the eastern Washington
prairie.

Holt's old man had said that quail will sit tight while you walk
right by, chukar will outrun you, and huns will do a bit of both. Best
to have a dog for all three. So Holt always had. First his father's, then
theirs together, now his alone. Father and son had kept their small
line of German shorthairs alive through careful breeding, once having to send their sire back to Minnesota in order to assure clean
stock. They'd mostly kept males and thus maintained the "pick-of-
the litter" rights that come with owning the stud.

Holt shot his father's 16-gauge Parker these days for everything,
and he still had some No. 10s his father had reloaded, shells that
were hell on quail, as was Kip, their youngest shorthair. It was Kip

that he loosed first the following morning at the northwest corner of the ranch, where a run of rose hips and olive followed a seep from a pair of beaver ponds. He had waited until the frost began to let go of the land, yet in the shadows of the draw the crispness still stung Holt's nose, and he fought the urge to shove his gunless hand into his Carhartt pockets as they began to hunt.

True enough he'd have walked past the first covey had it not been for Kip's sawed-off snout. As it was, the dog spun back from halfway up the wash, crossed the seep, then came up hard about twenty feet outside the rose hips and at the beginning of the sage. Holt knew he needed to cut the quail off from the thicket to afford himself any sort of respectable shooting, so he headed for the bush that fast. Kip was a hundred yards up the run, and although the dog had come on the quail fast, Holt always worried over early-season points and didn't want to waste time right then.

Once on Kip's side of the draw, Holt hugged the rose hips and covered the distance to the point in less than twenty paces. When the covey flushed, the quail split—half to the thick, half to the grassy, sage-blotched sidehill. He shouldered the gun but didn't fire, while marking the birds as they lit about the grass. He waited for the straggler that Kip had yet to give up on and killed it going away with the left barrel, after the bird had flushed right in his face before trying to give him a haircut, going just above his head.

Holt stroked the dog's back for a moment, then sent him to "find dead." After Kip pointed the stilled quail and Holt scooped it up and put the little cock bird in his game pouch, he told Kip, "Hunt!" while motioning the dog to the sidehill, where the birds would hold almost as tight in the bunchgrass as they would in the brushy draw—the shooting being all the difference.

That smooth, liquid, everlasting feeling—half expectation, half jubilance, and all confidence—moved inside Holt as he trailed the young dog, then watched the shorthair lock again tight to some sage that smelled sweet as prairie rain when he approached. The single bird turned into three, and Holt missed twice at the last quail as it banked away toward the sun.

"Huh," he grunted. Holt worked over his tobacco wad, spit, and said: "Good Kip. Good goin'. Hunt on."

The dog resumed his loping gate and tightened his quartering in the grass and sage until he froze again. This time Holt truly had to kick the sage to get the quail to flush. The bird almost made the rose hips and its family when it was cut short with the No. 10s. After Kip pointed dead and Holt gathered up the bird, he gave the "Hunt" command again.

Just where the grass ran out and the sage took over for keeps at the crest of the sidehill, Kip spun and shoved his nose into a clump of blue bunchgrass—his foreleg up, his ass square, and not a quiver of muscle.

"Bastard can hunt," Holt whispered to himself.

This bird made the hilltop but faltered terribly at the shot just beyond, and soon Holt had three plump quail in his game pouch. One more quail was all he would allow himself from this covey, and it took two more points before he had it. By which time his hands were warmed, his nose had quit running, and he was beginning to feel his toes come to life in his old leather hunting boots. He brought the young dog back to the seep, where it drank, and they rested a moment on the sunny side of the slope while Holt finished his chew.

...

It always amazed Holt when a woman as beautiful and bright as Karla got to liking him. What did someone like her want with a dirt farmer too stubborn to give up the only thing he knew how to do? And the reality was that he had married Becky two years prior and now had a baby fast on the way. There was nothing wrong with Becky by any stretch, other than the usual, though marriage hadn't exactly ever been Holt's idea. They'd spent some pretty fair years together, in which time he had remained faithful and mostly willing.

Now this faith was being seriously challenged for the first time, and it ate at his gut like a corkscrew being pulled in and out about where his navel was. The notion to run became more than nagging. It was more Karla's character—her knowledge and the integrity of her profession as a game biologist—than her cut body that wore on Holt. They shared too many of the same heartfelt beliefs about the land, animals, and farming to avoid mutual admiration. Was it their damned fault? They were just two people living two lives that had bumped into one another, not unlike the time Becky and he had lived years before. Holt felt a bit cursed—blessed and cursed all at once. And for nothing intentional even. But what about the pain it would cause?

...

Kip started to whine. "Ready boy?" said Holt. Without further thought, he brought the Parker to cradle once again, shifted his feed cap, and motioned the dog ahead. Magpies announced Kip's lead, as did a band of mule deer that headed like kangaroos over the hilltop to the south as man and dog continued up the draw. At the ponds themselves, now all frozen except where a group of teal and mallards were hiding, Kip found a new covey of quail. From this bunch Holt took four more birds over solid, single points. His game pouch now bumped comfortably against his rear as he made his way back to the pickup.

By the time he had let the two older dogs out, then put them back in and driven to another corner of the ranch where the fall rye was just now stooling out about six inches high in time for snow, a sharp breeze was stirring and keeping the sun from doing much good. Holt ate lunch on the tailgate after considering doing so inside the cab with the heater on. As he sat there with his back squared against one side of the truck bed, he knew he would never tire of this country, hard-boiled as it was.

He relished the contrast of the hardy, green fall grain against the otherwise fading landscape. He studied the staggered benches of flat land, then the sharp coulees that branched off down toward the mighty river some thousand feet below. The river that perhaps was a lake after nineteen dams, but was as much of a wild, out-of-control force as ever. If not more so now. As if in answer to man's trying to harness it, the river had actually turned monster-like.

Holt watched a pair of hunting harriers and took note of a golden eagle high, high above, riding the secret thermals that puffed about somewhere in the flawless sky. He sipped his coffee, chapped hands wrapped tight about the Thermos cup, and could have been happy to sit on into the afternoon. Alas, partridge wait-ed—waited for the shorthairs Pete and Hank to find them.

Why is it, Holt wondered as he slipped on his vest again, that you damn near wish for tragedy—wish for some sort of crisis to take hold just so that you have the license to take a day off from life? Like when his father had died five years earlier and Holt had taken his sweet time searching within himself whether he wanted to sell out or to keep on with the farming alone. It took that for him to step back, it seemed, and get a glimmer of objectiveness into his own damned life.

And now with his marriage threatened, a baby on the way, and about everything still up to him to decide the fate of, just as it had been in all his other relationships, this might be all the crisis he could stand. It was always his restlessness that threatened—threat-ened the good he had been working toward. What the hell was it that made him seek, search, never quite be content, and forever feel an old-time solace in that wayward prairie wind full of untouchable, inexplicable wonder like ragged autumn clouds, stiff moons, and southbound geese? Why did he take such comfort in lonesome? What was the attraction?

"Damn it to hell. Hunt, boys!"

And they did. Pete and Hank, brother dogs, cut across the spring wheat stubble, left for fallow, and banked toward the green-er new grain that stretched in dips and rises into the bright afternoon sun, the dogs themselves undulating across this landscape as if kin to that same prairie wind.

Holt felt his pace even out as the thick coffee went to work on the cold lunchtime tortillas. The easy rhythm of walking behind the dogs was a welcome change to the lifting, pulling, pushing of farming—the grease and grime of equipment, the shoveling of heavy grain he had been doing from dawn to dusk over the past six months. It was a one-man ranch show, with Becky helping when she could.

Pete skirted the ridge of the fall rye while Hank worked thirty yards or more down in the adjacent coulee. Holt split the difference whistling the pair of shorthairs back, then back until he saw Hank come up short. The dog's head was high and steady, but he was still hunting the breeze for location. Recognizing Hank's weak point and knowing that the birds were on the move, Holt whistled for Pete, who topped out about fifty yards ahead of Hank on the edge of the rye, then began quartering back toward his brother before he hit the brakes hard and wouldn't budge.

"Sweet," Holt muttered. Then, not to hesitate, he dropped some yards below the lower dog, which had moved up into a steadier point. "Easy, eeeasy boy," Holt said as he angled up, toward that spot of magic between the two staunch dogs.

Holt had barely made out the gray heads above the rocks when the huns flushed in a cacophony of chatter, trills, and echoes that nearly made him lose his balance. Finally, as the fans of rusty feathers smoothed out while staying in line with the ridge top, Holt was able to pull himself together enough to crumple one bird from the fringe of the covey. Then the birds set their wings, disappeared across the coulee, and were gone as gone around the next bench to who-the-hell-knows. How such a sure thing that fast had turned into fleeting opportunity baffled Holt as much as when it had happened for the very first time.

Pete pointed the dead bird and Holt picked it up. He felt its lofty warmth in his hand, then held it to his cheek as the breeze cut under his shirt cuffs and the sun fought to stay high overhead. He had shot maybe a thousand huns since he first started hunting behind his father, yet every single bird somehow seemed an untouchable perfection. As if you could hold it dead in your hand but you could never claim its precise appearance and spirit. Any more than you could claim the land by simply sowing seed and loving the seasons, even though as mortals that might be the best you could do.

"Nice job, boys. Damn nice job. Hunt!"

And onward they went, forgetting about the big covey that just put the slip on them and keeping their line between the green grain and coulee, their noses tight to the northerly stir.

The dogs legged out for some time, never cutting any scent. Then they ran out of the coulee and green grain, hitting the stubble from that year's spring wheat. This field bordered a run of bunchgrass that was one of the grazing plots in June for the fifty head of Hereford cattle that Holt still owned. He ran the cows in here for about three weeks—and no more—each June, so the stand remained vigorous and full throughout the dry summer.

...

That craving, hungry, melancholy feeling was working on Holt again. He imagined enjoying being a father and sharing that with Becky, and he couldn't imagine being without Becky at all. Yet he couldn't pass up beauty for beauty's sake either, and his heart reached for this. He shunned the thought of not being able to explore Karla—not ever being able to hike, talk, hunt, and yes, in the end, maybe lie with her. This thought of *never, ever* hurt about as badly as the thought of abandoning his soon-to-be family. He'd have to move out, is all. Or stay and move in—squelching all his heartfelt urges to better concentrate on his family. Exactly how did you do that? How did you stomp out your longings long enough for them to dissipate? Did you remain strong in the hope of forgetting? Did you—or could you—ever forget, or did trying simply make it worse? That he was conjuring up Karla made things difficult to be sure. Or was it just the same old ubiquitous Holt, closing in on forty now and circling right back to twenty.

The birds flushed in wild directions about the time Holt was getting sullied up good. He got over sorry just in time to mark a handful of birds out in the grass. Holt had lost track of the dogs and was frustrated all over until he glimpsed Hank's tail locked still in the stubble, with Pete frozen by his side. Holt's heart rose up into his throat as he crossed out of the grass toward the dogs.

The lone partridge flushed in a racket and didn't stand a chance against gold stubble and cold blue sky. Holt could see the bird so defined—could see its eyes, could sense its panic, and could damn near slow its wingbeats down. He was still marveling at its clarity as he touched the front trigger, followed by the rear. The bird never missed a beat on its way to the far and never land below the field.

Holt stuttered—laughed even. Hank rolled a curious eye over on him. "Christ on a crutch, boys. It don't get any better. I believe I'm screwed up."

It got better. His hard-running, self-honed, free and lucky dogs would not falter, and they soon pinned the bunch of huns in the grass so that Holt had a chance to double on the next rise. He came up empty but then killed three singles in a row, two over Pete, the third over Hank when the dogs located the bigger half of the covey— some twenty birds—along the grassy terrace. Every hun was full up with hard, red wheat left from the harvest.

When Hank pointed the third bird, Holt had felt the groove coming, sensed that easy gate, that strength in his legs as he zigzagged up to the point. He saw nothing but a shape that kept swinging as it left a puff of feathers behind—a shape that became visible over the gun's twin barrels only after he released his cheek from the marred, worn, and still-solid gunstock.

How he loved it—that tangy smell of moistening air, the smoky flavor of brittle grasses as they lifted to life again after a beating of summer heat, loved the sharpness of the land. Most of all he loved his dogs, which now sat with him on the edge of the stubble and drank from the water bottle he had packed along. Drank between pants and closed their eyes in satisfaction as they licked Holt's salty hands. He already missed them—already couldn't bear the thought of shooting and burying when the time would come some years from now. As if he had to start preparing himself for that pain this soon. As if that was the price for loving deeply, if not often, and always with an honest heart.

Holt was mighty pleased just then to have followed his hunting heart all this time—the need, want, lust of pursuing these wild birds in this free land. And to have spent so much time training dogs that it nearly became innate, so that now when his life took that turn and obligation mounted, it seemed to all come back with even stronger desire and grace.

The afternoon was clear enough that he could see the Cascades far to the west, already white, aged, austere, and brilliant over the dry and fading land before him. They appeared as new life in this dying season, for no other reason, perhaps, than they had changed by putting on winter's cloak without reluctance and had gained power by it.

It struck Holt for the first time that this truly was the season when the mountains ruled and all else rested. Those craggy peaks were sucking the sun down at a sudden rate that moment, and although he had again worked up a mild sweat, Holt hoped the snow would hold off a couple more weeks because he had some hunting to do. Christ, fall had just begun! Where'd all that in-between time get to? That time between the good season and the rest: *summer.* This feeling of no return caught him off-guard so that he wanted the weather right then to never leave. He wanted a month of it, yet he could feel the land's growing calm and knew that he was just falling into its traces today, while winter damn well might claim it tomorrow. I should have started earlier, he guessed. But there was the ranch . . .

He thought of the youngest dog, Kip, back in the pickup and he recognized the time for heading that way. He had packed his sleeping bag and stuff for the night. He was going to drink beer, grill birds on the fire, and fall asleep under the stars to the wood's warm crackle with the dogs curled all around him. He wanted to get the fire together before dark, get the dogs all watered and fed so he could relax before drawing the birds, then roasting them alongside some potato and beans and cheese-filled tortillas. God, he was hungry and thirsty all at once.

He would camp right about where the truck was parked, by the edge of the fall rye, at the top of the aspen run that had survived even the last three years of drought. He would lie full and sated under those aspen and listen to the tenuous rustle of leaves in the evening breeze—to that haunting, familiar, age-old sound that could make him damn near want a tepee.

Holt felt stiff when he rose, his right knee a little swollen, his back creaky but, considering his life up to forty, he figured he could be a fair bit worse so he fell in behind the dogs again. They weren't yet content to be done, and they picked up another covey of huns about a quarter-mile from the truck. Holt had a good whack at the rise but held off, knowing that he had birds enough for dinner and breakfast, and that he might or might not hunt them tomorrow. He was pleased to watch the huns fan out over the green rye, to watch them rise then scoot down the coulee to the west, leaving nothing but distant snowy peaks with the sun perched on them and the far-off yip of old coyote and the evening chill and the silence of their leaving accentuated by the coming twilight. A solitary cock pheasant crowed from down in the aspen. They'd get some pheasant tomorrow too, Holt and his dogs.

Back at the pickup, Kip was more than thrilled to see them; all the dogs bounced around Holt until he had dug out their food, water, and one perfect beer. Dusk may well create lonesome of its own accord, but Holt missed Becky, though he had been thinking mostly about Karla all day. He even missed the homestead. No shame in missing familiarity he figured.

These feelings passed as soon as the full of night fell and a sliver of moon set in the west and the fire crackled. As soon as the beer took hold, and the birds were cleaned and seasoned and sitting on the tailgate ready for the fire, the dogs sprawled around his feet and his bootlaces undone. All of tomorrow's worries would be up bright and early to greet him. Scamper as they would, they could wait until then, for at that moment, Holt had all he truly desired within arms' reach.

He wondered if the day would come when he'd share some of all this with his children.

Treed

The birds, as usual, caught Tuckerman and Chew off guard. Dumb ones. "Woods chickens," as folks in parts of Maine and Canada sometimes called them. And even though Tuck had heard his Brittany's bell stop, he was—as usual—peeing.

They came up in ones and twos, confusing Chew. Tuck himself barely got things shut off in time to take a long poke with the left barrel at the last and closest bird flying broadside some forty yards off. It was a tall shot for his 28-gauge, but the bird acted odd as it glided into a spruce top.

Venture, the Brittany, pursued. She stopped under the tree and started her high-pitched barking. That's what she always cut loose with when she spied a treed grouse. She stayed insistent and wouldn't leave. Both barrels loaded again, Tuck cautiously made his way toward the tree, anticipating the overhead flush. He remembered making this impossible shot only twice. However, when he got to the base of the spruce, the bird didn't budge. Maybe this was a dumb one after all?

Then he saw the bird lying near the top of the tree. He could scarcely make out the limp head and firm wings pointing skyward, confirming a dead bird, indeed. Venture never lied.

"Boy that ol' twenty-eight sure is a hard hitter, huh, Chew?" Tuck was forever talking up the small gun, particularly whenever he made an exceptional poke—which is to say about once a year.

"I dunno," Chew said. "I think the sucker's so dumb you just scared it to death."

For some time now, they'd heard how easy it was to shoot

northern "pa'tridge." (Piles of birds . . . dumb as a stone . . . shoot 'em from the truck window with a .22.) So finally Chew and Tuck had decided it'd be worth a trip "up north." Not only were the limits more generous in Canada for both grouse and woodcock, but the season started a couple of weeks earlier than it did stateside. With a good working dog, it should prove a cinch: pa'tridge shootin' to someday tell the grandchildren about as they made wide, sweeping gestures with their briar-proof hands, sitting and rocking beside the barrel stove.

It was Tuck's idea, and he knew Chew would be game because he generally was for any new adventure involving guns or skis or beer (preferably all three). Tuck had got hold of him and after loading the beat-up Dodge truck with assorted gear, they'd left New Hampshire for Quebec in mid-September, on a growing harvest moon.

After two nights of sleeping in the pickup bed in rain and snow, the boys were into the third day of gunning. Save for the bird that Venture pointed immediately after Tuck let her out at the very first covert—while he and Chew fumbled for their guns through a disorganized pile of stuff—they hadn't so much as laid eyes on a grouse. They'd flushed plenty but had only heard the wings of the birds breaking thick foliage ahead of Venture's bell. They'd managed to scratch down enough woodcock for meals, in a god-awful maze of lead-proof cover. That was all.

Now Venture, still grumpy from the long drive up and the lack of woods chickens, finally had a dead one. Sort of.

The tree the bird lay in actually hung from another dead spruce—one trunk for two trees. Chew came up behind Tuck, who looked at Venture, pointed up, and said, "Fetch." The dog gave Tuck a passive, coy look that soon he would never be able to shake. She'd quit barking and was daintily just sitting there. At once, Tuck quit laughing.

"Now what, Chew?"

"Dunno. Think we can shake it out of there?"

"I'd sooner try that than climb. Damn bird's dead as a spent shell. Got to get it."

They put their guns down in a safe place and grabbed hold of the tree trunk and started shaking it for all they were worth. The corpse didn't move. Tuck found some chunks of busted wood and started hurling them in an effort to dislodge the thing. Not a chance. Soon it became apparent as to what the boys must do.

Seeing that bird way up there made Tuck feel about the way he did the time he didn't, for some reason, have the dog along and had shot some black ducks he ended up swimming to the middle of the pond for last November. Flat-out dumb.

Tuck didn't necessarily like heights to begin with, and the more he eyed the rotted limbs above, the more he wished he'd missed the grouse. However, a dead bird is a dead bird and so far these grouse hadn't come easy despite their lesser reputation. Tuck swore he noticed a twinkle in Venture's eye as he shed his vest and started up the tree.

About every third limb broke—and his heart skipped a beat each time. Chew stood below helplessly watching, and when Tuck got maybe fifteen feet up, Venture took off hunting again. She hadn't gone far before her bell stopped.

"Venture's got a bird," Chew said. "What should I do?"

"Shoot it. No sense letting any get away," Tuck assured his partner while continuing to climb. He had a tight grip on a solid limb, or so he thought until it gave way about the time Chew shot. Somehow, Tuck was able to catch himself by quickly pinching the stubby trunk with his legs. In so doing, he sensed something sharp stab him in a not-so-desirable spot, and he let out more of a squeak than a groan.

"Dead bird," Chew yelled. Venture's bell started working again as Tuck climbed higher.

"She's got another one," Chew hollered.

"Shoot it," Tuck shouted back. Another limb cracked at the shot, but Tuck had hold of the tree itself with both hands this time.

"Dead bird!" Again, the bell tolled. Tuck was about two-thirds of the way to his bird.

Truth to tell, he didn't mind climbing trees; he'd done it as a kid all the time: maples, oaks, and even swinging birches. But if a person had a choice, the last tree he'd pick to "shinny" was a northern red spruce. It was similar to pawing for a golf ball in a rose hedge. Both Tuck's forearms bled steadily now, and he'd torn his wool coat at least once. However, so long as he didn't look down, he was still feeling as if he'd make the retrieve.

"She's got another one!" Chew shouted from a distant stand of young beech trees.

It appeared that Venture had found the bunch of young grouse that the boys had originally flushed by peeing, the one that had put Tuck in this predicament to begin with. "Jesus Christ!" he cried.

"What?" Chew shouted. "I said, she's got another one."

"Shoot the sonuva . . ." This time Tuck held his position in the spruce until Chew fired.

"Dead bird," came Chew's command to the dog.

Good, Tuck thought. There can't be but a couple more. He heard Venture's bell trail off, then come back around. She hunted better for Chew than she ever had for Tuck. The whole thing was pretty as hell to watch: three points, three dead grouse, in three minutes. At the moment, though, Tuck was thirty feet off the ground; he was running out of good limbs fast and had other things to visualize. He had stayed in pretty good shape year round but hadn't done much tree climbing lately. Good thing he never lacked for stubbornness.

Venture and Chew came back just as Tuck closed in on the grouse's grave. Tuck looked down because he knew better, and there sat Venture, cool as ice at the base of the tree.

Chew, who didn't get his name from smoking, stood beside the Brittany working over a huge wad of Redman tobacco. He looked up and smiled, allowing streams of dark juice to run out of the corners of his mouth.

"She's got you right where she wants you," he said. "Treed—after all these years. Gonna get you back for all those times you missed easy shots after making her sit in the truck all day. And making her eat when she didn't feel like it. And not getting a fire built last night. She has eight seasons worth of spite built up, and she's collecting on it right now," he laughed.

Tuck could sense that Chew was feeling smart, having gone three for three and all, like some leadoff batter in the last game of the World Series. But Tuck was feeling pretty victorious himself, so the truth ran off him like rain. Near the top of the tree, Tuck was now face to face with the dead grouse, kind of enjoying the nice view from up there: the sea of orange and reds rolling on forever below as the changing season's reward. No one else in the world had that exact view just then—not even Venture. "Ah . . . the crafty woods chicken," he piped up triumphantly, reaching for the bird.

Just then—suddenly, horribly—the bird's tufted head reared up and stared him straight in the eye. Then the grouse exploded from the tree, leaving nothing but spruce needles and a stray tail feather in Tuck's groping hand.

"Blast it!" he wailed and fell back, crashing down five feet or more to where his butt snubbed up on a busted limb. Chew had previously laid his gun down, and this furthered the bird's escape. Anger, amazement, good fortune—a series of emotions raced through Tuck at once. Venture started barking and running in tight circles below, jumping up and down, excited as a pup. Tuck was close to tears and petrified to move an inch.

What seemed like a month passed. Then slowly, ever so slowly, Tuck focused again, studied the limbs below, gathered himself, and eased into his descent.

By the time he made the ground, he'd broken most all the limbs from the spruce tree. Two major chunks of flesh hung from his forearms, his flannel shirt was ripped in several places, and he had burns and scratches and was sticky with pitch from head to toe. Chew acted equally astonished.

"Why didn't you kill that thing?" Tuck demanded.

"Thought you already had—with the good ol' twenty-eight," Chew said. "These French grouse sure are dumb. They die and don't even know it. Kinda like a cat, I guess. I can't believe it. Did you see that?"

"*See it?!?* I guess the hell. Damned thing tried to kill me—baiting me clear up there and all." Then suddenly, a more frightening thought struck Tuck. He screwed his eyes shamefully over at Venture, who immediately turned away. Could it be? Had she known all along? What a nasty ploy!

"Venture," Tuck said in his lowest voice. "How could you, girl?" She slunk over behind Chew, acting as if she had just bumped a bird or snatched one from the barbecue. Tuck felt so alarmed that he could barely speak. Finally, he retained enough courage to put on his vest and pick up his gun. At his request, "the boys" didn't bother going after that particular bird again. Instead, they headed back for the road.

Continuing along the road apiece, Tuck refused to say a word to Venture. Much to the dog's satisfaction, he just let her hunt and she soon had two more decent points.

When the first grouse flushed, Tuck froze stiff as an oak. A sudden flash ran through him as it had when he'd started to fall in the spruce tree, and he trembled. The flash was not one of excitement, as it used to be, but more the shock of horror, like the time he'd walked proudly up the aisle in a Catholic wedding procession and had looked down to see his tuxedo fly gaping wide.

When the second bird flushed and Chew shot it, Tuck's nerves made him want to give up breakfast for an early lunch.

Tuck stopped by the stream on their way back to the truck and scraped off some of the crusted wounds, before dunking his head in the cold mountain water. When they reached their campsite, Chew said he'd fix lunch and opened a can of beans, spread some on a piece of bread, and handed it to Tuck. "Wanta beer to go with that? You're looking kinda pale," said his friend.

Tuck just stared at the pathetic fire pit from the night before, when he'd failed to produce a lasting flame out of swamp alder and ether. The singed twigs lay as reminders of how perturbed Venture had been after watching patiently for half an hour in the falling snow. In the end, the dog had turned away, deciding—once again—that her master was some poor excuse for a woodsman.

All at once, Tuck began to feel that this land was hollow, if not surreal. "No," he said. "I think I better keep on hunting this afternoon, till I get over this. We ought to try down by that stream. I'm for some woodcocking: small trees, small birds. Help even out the day a bit. These woods chickens up here are different. Gonna punch the next guy who tells me how easy they are. Those that talk of it must never have tried 'em"

"I dunno. That was strange, no two ways about it," Chew said. "But there's most of a limit in my pouch that says a lot of 'em act all right."

"Fact is, Chew," Tuck went on, staring at the blackened pile of alder without really paying his friend any regard, "they're as challenging as any bird I've seen. They're downright scary. I'm not sure if this is what they mean by rough shootin' or not, but if we're not real careful from here on, these here woods chickens might just ruin my dog."

Passing

Mike and I were in "The Dentist's Blind" the day Bob died.

At least this is what I often referred to as his blind—a soundly constructed, wooden, four-man hide that steps down with the slope of the long island's point near the top of the refuge. A slatted floor allows water to drain from wet waders and dogs. Burlap walls and a wire roof woven with reeds blend it into the rocks and brush. The hinged front is thatched with vegetation, as well. It's a long and narrow space with a bench comfortable enough to sleep on. However, Bob and his partners did not build such a fine blind for sleeping. Here, what's left of the mighty river makes a big, sweeping bend before straightening out on its dam-riddled journey to the Pacific. Here the blind was strategically placed for the shooting of ducks and geese. And Bob's companions shot a lot of both—particularly geese.

I hardly ever hunted this blind. The times I got the inclination to, I always called Bob first to see if he had plans to hunt there himself the following day. "Go for it," he'd always say. "Knock 'em dead."

We usually didn't, but when a lot of birds were moving, they decoyed well: mallards, divers, geese. And I think those who helped build the blind knew how to set their spread better than I did. My luck came in other parts of the refuge. In my earlier years, there was hardly ever anyone else around. As Bob said, the whole area was a great fowling secret.

This morning Mike and I had come for geese. We didn't always get loads of ducks at The Dentist's Blind, but it was as good a place to hunt geese over water as any. The day we hunted was after Christmas, and the Columbia River had gone all gray with snow that flowed from the plateau to the north. From inside the blind, situated right at the river's edge, you could sense the magnitude of this huge water, despite the fact that its power had been transformed. You could see the current swirl and break around the point, tugging at the stony banks, at the same time making the decoys dance to life.

Eagles worked the water and shoreline constantly, hoping to catch an unsuspecting widgeon or coot or fish. Every so often, we'd see a great fish, too—an almost monsterlike head breach the surface. We'd skip a breath and remark: Damn, if that wasn't a fish! But we never knew exactly what we'd seen: a steelhead, a chinook, or just a carp. It felt all safe and sound because of the meandering channel that separated the island from the mainland and the adjacent alfalfa field, but we didn't have to motor far from the blind to feel lost in the big water. And if the wind picked up, we knew that channel could save our lives.

On the good days, when scores of divers were in the area, we would often see them head up the long shore of the island toward the blind. Sometimes they'd hone in on our blocks the first pass. We'd keep the front of the blind closed until whoever was on the downriver side called the shot. Then we'd push open the front to a flock of redheads, cans, or bluebills straight out over the spread. Other times, divers would pass upriver out of range, only to swing back minutes later and actually set into the blocks from the other side. Mallards were drawn to the slow channel in the lee of the island, and widgeon were often flitting about. The geese were a story unto themselves. They came from every direction, acted differently every time, but seemed always to be passing by the island's tip on their way to the "off-limits" field of alfalfa. Bob said he and his friends shot more than fifty geese here one year. I believe him still.

...

A moving mist kept daybreak at bay a bit longer than usual at this darkest time of the year. We could hear a distant goose occasionally, but this was nothing like the normal cacophony. Mike was staring straight out at the bluff on the far shore, the one that always made it tough to see incoming ducks. "Is that a flock of birds or just the mist?" he wondered aloud.

"Where?"

"Way up over the plateau. Give me the binoculars."

"Probably just the mist," I said, handing him the glasses.

"Hard to say. Looks like a damn ghost."

"I've seen lots of strange stuff this time of year down here. Especially at daybreak."

"Those are birds! Holy shit, look at them all! A frigging ball of birds."

He was right, an absolute dark flock oddly swarming north—quickly. "Gotta be ducks," I said. "Nothing else would be traveling that fast. Hey, there is another wad right behind them. And another."

"Where the hell are they coming from?" asked Mike.

"Where are they going? I wondered. "Imagine if that ball set into our dekes! There's gotta be a thousand birds in each bunch!"

"Two thousand. There's another ball. That's the strangest thing."

"That must be what they call 'duck smoke,' " I said.

Across the plateau, nearly a mile off, four oblong flocks of ducks moved with conviction. They were headed up the smaller river valley, and very little separated them from just another duck-hunter's apparition. Then they were gone, leaving Mike and me dumbfounded, staring at nothing but the water and no birds. Silence returned.

"What about Bob? I just can't believe it," I said.

"He's going down fast. Once the cancer's in your liver, things go pretty quickly."

"To think he never knew till three months ago. Makes me sick."

"Hard to say which is worse, knowing for a long time or not knowing till it's too late."

Preferably neither, I thought to myself. I still couldn't quite grasp it.

In my more selfish moments, I thought not of Bob's family but of my own loss—of being cheated. Cheated because I hadn't spent the time with Bob that I'd been hoping to. He was one of those rare folks whom, whenever I saw him, I wanted to get to know more—wanted to be around his positive spirit. Two springs earlier, soon after a Ducks Unlimited banquet, we finally connected on dinner at our place. My wife and I remarked after Bob and his wife left how genuine they seemed, how it felt so right to get to know good people and to connect on the warmest of levels. We looked forward to forming a stronger friendship.

I first came to know Bob through his dentistry, soon after I'd moved to town, where I knew nobody. His office was full of DU prints and other telltale signs of his love for nature. Talk between us soon fell to hunting. At that point, I was a bit on the run: dogless for the first time, three thousand miles from my New England homeland, and unsure what my future held. Bob's immediate enthusiasm and kindness ran through me like a long, fresh drink of mountain water. He told me how great the bird hunting was in the West. He encouraged me and later informed me about a couple of good areas to try. Little did I know what a beginning this was—that what he so easily told me would keep me from making a good living from then on and that just when I thought my birding fever was cooling, it was actually cranking up more than ever.

To his credit, Bob never showed me exactly where or how to hunt certain areas along the river. I became a better hunter for having to figure out these things on my own. That spring I got a retriever pup, and soon enough I spent as much time investigating as doing.

During the following years, I'd often hear Bob and his partners shooting up at the head of the refuge, and I would comfortably know it was they who were taking the birds. I in turn had my couple of spots and was doing the same.

Much later, as I was standing in the blind Bob had built, blankly looking out at the empty water, it occurred to me that though it seemed my dentist and I had hunted "together" quite frequently, we never once had. Herein lay more of an understanding: a shared experience from having been in the same area on the same days and loving the same things about the whole mystery of wildfowl, of the north, of the big autumn skies, and of the jewels in them.

The sunrises, snowstorms, dogs, and lore were mutually felt, so that when we ran into each other at the hidden boat launch or shared the occasional visit to our respective blinds, we could give to one another that knowing smile, and few words needed to be exchanged. Some days the shooting was undeniably hot and we might show off an exceptional canvasback or pintail or goose. On other days, the gunning would be slow, but the time afield was always good—particularly before the refuge began to see more use and before the couple of mild winters and before the stretch when it seemed windy a lot.

One early November day a few years prior, Mike and I were hunting one of the lower islands on the river while Bob and his steady partner were up in their spot. The November sky was sharp and blue and full of puffy wind clouds moving over the plateau to the north. The wind built up as the morning aged, and with it came a fair shot of birds. Mike and I were enjoying some fine mixed shooting on redheads, mallards, and widgeon—but no geese. The day was righteous for the turn of the season, and our dogs were working well together.

By early afternoon we were filled out with fourteen birds and figuring we ought to escape the wind while we could. As we were picking up, Bob and his partner showed up on the lee side of the island. They were grinning. The bow of their boat was full of geese, though they had only three or four ducks. Bob peered onto our bow, looked up, and said: "We got 'em today, didn't we?"

They helped us pick up our wind-torn spread, and we slowly watched each other into the safety of the channel and back to the launch ramp—the only two groups on this entire section of river that afternoon.

Bob and I talked about that day—and others like it—at the DU banquet in the spring, We talked about how lucky we were to have such
good, uncrowded gunning. Then he would hook me into another roll
of raffle tickets because you couldn't say no to Bob in his jeans, sport
coat, and duck tie.

Not surprisingly, I was in Bob's dental office on the day I needed
him most. The previous evening I'd shattered a top molar on one of
those fine pieces of No. 1 steel we used to shoot. The following day—
Wednesday and the day before Thanksgiving—was a goose day. Of
course, Bob was out hunting. Around noontime I called his residence
because he had the number listed for emergencies. Luckily his wife
was home, but she confirmed my suspicions. She said she would let
him know of my predicament as soon as he got home.

At two o'clock, Bob called. My tooth was killing me as only an
injured chomper can. "Meet me down at the office in twenty minutes," he said.

Bob showed up in waders. He had no staff there on Wednesdays
so the prep work, mixing, and cleaning were all up to him. We were
in his office for two hours that afternoon. I'd often suspected that
dentists were behind the steel-shot movement all along, and the latest mishap to my pearly whites only furthered this suspicion—a
notion I more than once had shared with Bob. During that afternoon
he joked about it, but he mostly concentrated on extracting three big
chunks of my molar, then molding half of a tooth out of some mira-
cle putty that he then bonded onto what was left of mine. When he
finished, he said I'd need to get a crown for the tooth—someday.

Each year or so for the following four or five, Bob would patch
up my patch whenever it got worn down, send me out of the office
with no charge, saying: "Someday, boy, you oughta get a crown on
that."

Now I'll never get a tooth crown from Bob. Now I'll never be
able to thank him enough for his work, for his small-town kindness,
for letting me in on some great hunting, for his sharing the world of

ducks with me. Now I won't ever get to hunt in a blind together the way we'd hoped. I'll miss just waving to him as we pass on the road, knowing certain ducking secrets we know.

What gets to me is the prematurity of it—the shutoff of a long-lasting friendship never to blossom. Of daybreaks never shared, of beliefs felt, yet of connections never quite consummated to the satisfaction of those of us left.. As if Bob's departure was the unwarranted burning of a community gift.

I've spent some hollow days out on the river while gunning for ducks, alone with just my own demons. I've felt the fog press down with illusion and silence and a rabid unforgiveness. Fairness is not always part of this life, therefore kindness must reap its own rewards. Believing this allows me to believe that Bob took almost as many treasures with him as he left behind. Like the unspoken truths between us, like the stirring mysteries of autumn's hawkish wind.

I'm left to think Bob would be pleased to know that Mike and I were in his blind the day he so suddenly took flight. Hard to say whether or not he had anything to do with those ghostlike balls of birds passing to the north that morning, but I'm not saying we were alone, either. And now it occurs to me—soothes me even—that though I never actually hunted with Bob, hereafter I'll always be hunting with him.

To be sure, next season, we'll all be gunning new ground.

Winter River

Come winter, I'll take a river
clear, cold, mountain born
lined in cottonwoods
kept by fields.

Mallards, pintails, snow
funnel down the north wind
straight from a somewhere prairie
to these strewn rapids
and long, quiet pools
freezing only at zero,
puffing restless mists,
driving late ducks.

Raucous fowl regale
feeding for what's ahead,
hungry from what's behind.
My Lab and I watch
tucked close to a brush line
savoring the minutes
till the time now has come:
I stand,
the dog tightens,
the winter river roars, and
wings of current permeate.

The Hunted

Bill cradled the worn double-barreled shotgun, as a warm memory kept gently in the back of his mind. It was his father's gun; besides a telescope, it was the only remnant of the Iowa farm Bill grew up on. Now fifteen hundred miles farther west and forty years later, the cool of the morning reminded him of those crimson boyhood hours spent hunting in the company of his father.

He studied the long shadows of early dawn sagging upon the brittle grasses. Though the air was sharp, Bill sensed a distant haziness, as if the midday heat had proceeded the sun and was already settling into the high meadows. Beyond them, the sharp mountains still hugged patches of old snow in their deepest crevices. He heard a meadowlark call softly to the sun. He failed to locate the bird but envisioned it perched on a clump of bitterbrush, its head thrown back in a gesture to relieve the consonance from its swollen throat. He heard the bees gather: a chorus of humming workers before another busy day. A half-moon hung high in the growing, western sky. September, he felt, was a hell of a poor month for dying.

But they had told him he was doing just that. "They" being doctors like himself. To not believe them would be betraying his own knowledge, his own life. But he thought that to give in and die might be a greater betrayal still. They told him the stomach cancer had grown, yet he'd hiked with his dog to the ridge top before daylight this morning, the tests be damned. It had taken Bill a long time to cover the mile, but he was none the worse for it. He felt better than he had that spring after completing the first months of chemotherapy, when the doctors had thought he'd beat the original tumor.

Bill leaned against a boulder behind him, his shoulders snug in suspenders that reached around him like long, comforting arms from some bygone time. Now he knew why his father always wore them: the suspenders seemed to hold a man when there was little else. Bill's sweat began to dry and he wiped his glasses and he drank from the water bottle before offering it to the young setter. Then Bill watched as she gulped anxiously at the nipple, like an infant would at its mother's. For the first time he felt glad that he and Hannah hadn't any children. Already there was enough to miss.

He thought of how he and Hannah had only lived in their country home for a year now. It had been their dream for nearly the entire thirty years they had worked in Seattle, where they'd met while attending medical school. Neither were ever from the city. The closest town to the farm in Iowa where Bill was born had a population of three hundred. Three hundred people who had pulled together, pitched what little they could afford into one pool, and helped Bill's folks send their only child to school. Bill had never forgotten this and he missed the town that had given him the rare opportunity to try something besides farming. But he had met Hannah in Seattle and had stayed.

Although they'd spent their entire careers in the city, there was always something missing—something in the distance. Bill ran his hands down the length of his shotgun and glanced over the far side of the ridge and down at the aspen grove below, which was tinged with early-autumn yellow. He smiled, realizing the significance of sticking up for and pursuing what he believed in. An odd sense of wiseness struck him. Old and wise he smirked. But at sixty he didn't feel old.

In some ways Bill felt as young as when Hannah had begun her practice in the family-planning field at the same hospital where he used to work. Before Roe versus Wade, back when family planning was still a filthy phrase. She soon tired of the hospital's constricted and often insensitive ways, and she left, after Bill, for many of the same reasons. And, like him, she struggled in eventually establishing her own clinic.

This morning Bill came to realize what he and Hannah had been working toward all those selfless years when he had made house calls and had taken on patients who couldn't pay and had looked on everybody in the city as family. Through their steady giving, Bill and Hannah had actually been striving for a different peace than that which they'd conjured within, a peace just as boundless but one that came from somewhere outside. So when they found the abandoned ranch in the eastern foothills of the Cascades, they bought it with little hesitation.

Bill stuck his hand in his vest pocket and sifted the shotshells through his fingers. He was going for grouse today, following the dog as he'd followed his father's setters as early as he could remember. He was startled right then by the realization that he hadn't really hunted since leaving the farm. He'd always seen the land in animated fashion when he went with his father and the dogs. And the importance he felt when his father first invited him along was still with Bill today, even though it was another two years before his father allowed him to share the gun.

The first and only winter he and Hannah had spent at the ranch, Bill sat nights gazing at stars through his childhood telescope, while Hannah started in on all the books she'd been meaning to read for the past thirty years—books that eventually inspired her to scratch away at some prose of her own. The skies here on the dry side of the mountains were pristine and reminiscent of the deep autumn skies Bill and his father walked under while returning through the harvested cornfields at twilight after hunting. Bill hadn't seen constellations this clear since and had guessed they might no longer exist.

He sorted the shells in his pocket and debated which pair to load. His father had told him always to begin the hunt with a pair of shells that were brass-up, for this would encourage the day's shooting. Bill's fingers paused on three shells that stood that way. He pulled out two from the front of his pocket and placed them with care into the gun's worn breech. His plan was to intercept the grouse on their way up from the aspen, where they'd roosted, to where they liked to feed before noon on the hilltop. But grouse were grouse, and hell if he knew whether they were there at all.

Bill let the dog start hunting, and they eased off the hill. As they worked down the north slope, Bill saw the first sunlight touch the distant peaks, turning them from purple to blue. He knew he and the dog would have the cool of the hill's shadow for no more than an hour, then the heat of the open day would be upon them and they'd have to watch for snakes. Bill wasn't supposed to exert himself, anyway.

What the hell? he thought. And Bill was almost caught up in the music of his hunting dog's quartering back and forth across the hillside when he suddenly became annoyed at Hannah for not accompanying him this morning. She had earlier in the month, toting a scratch pad and binoculars, while Bill carried the water and gun. He recalled that on the third day out they actually got a bird. And he remembered how that evening they had giggled while trying to agree on the best way to cook the grouse—both of them having done it so long ago. That had been first thing in the month, before the latest tests had revealed a much newer and larger tumor. One that would require a trip to the city for radical, internal treatment, and for an indefinite period of time. They would leave tomorrow.

When the cancer was first discovered, neither Bill nor Hannah could understand, though they'd seen it happen to others too many times. The first night, as they lay in bed, Hannah in a soft yet professional way had turned to Bill and said, "We'll get through this. We won't pretend it doesn't exist. We must accept it and persevere, as we've told so many before."

And after the first round of treatments, when Bill was hollow and ragged from the searing radiation, Hannah buzzed about with the determination and sureness of any great and hopeful nurse. She went to the local health market and bought him good teas and vitamins and the freshest produce available. She made him eat when his body said no. She read to him from Pound and Frost and Whitman in front of the fire. She built him up before each treatment, describing all the hikes they'd take come spring, when he was well again. And he would again be well, she asserted.

Toward the end of the twice-a-week treatments, Bill began to sense some improvement. Save for the lack of hair, he looked okay within a week after completing the regimen. He donned a baseball cap and resumed a sort of familiar life.

By March, Bill and Hannah were back skiing into town for breakfast. And when the waitress, Judy, asked them how Bill was, they told her the truth: He had a tumor in his stomach but they thought he was ahead of it.

At the post office Bill ran into his neighbor Randy. It was Randy's son who had gotten his pant leg caught in the driveshaft of a hay baler one day that summer. In a panic, Randy's wife had called Bill, who was able to gather some medical odds and ends and arrive within ten minutes. Randy had been close enough to see the accident and shut the baler down, but not before the driveshaft had ripped the skin from the leg. Bill was able to sedate the boy and staunch the profuse bleeding, which likely saved his life.

Bill's rough-cut neighbor was forever grateful and said as much that day at the post office. The two men talked easily, even about the cancer. "I wouldn't believe I was sick," Bill told Randy. "Except the doctors say so."

"Damn doctors don't know anything," Randy chortled with a sly grin. He laid his huge hand on Bill's shoulder and squared him in the eyes. "We'll be over to fix up those corrals soon as Hannah gets her horses. Meantime we're thinkin' of ya'"

This morning it was people like Randy who were killing him—people he so looked forward to spending the rest of his life with, people like those he'd grown up with. How had this chance become so fleeting?

To be sure, by being up front about the cancer with his neighbors and townsfolk, Bill had felt his courage grow. No sense hiding it. And there never was doubt in Hannah's mind that the illness would pass. Bill had this to stand on. Yet this morning Hannah had sent him hunting alone. It was rare they ever did anything apart, particularly now. They'd gotten firewood together the first fall and taken long walks over the cooling October terrain. They had skied the hills of the ranch the remainder of the winter and then, come April, put in a garden. Randy and his boy had helped them fix up the corrals, and Hannah had gotten her pair of horses. Bill had bought the setter. The three of them had ridden deep into the mountains to escape the summer heat. And then there was the hunting.

These days, the way Hannah at once became quiet bothered Bill, hinting that she might think he was actually going to die. "What do the damn doctors know?" he said aloud. And right then Bill saw a hawk hanging in an air current overhead. He noticed that the dog had stopped, and then he saw a grouse hunkered low under some sage as the predatory shadow passed above, circling round and round. Whether the grouse was aware of the dog, as well, Bill did not know. At once he identified with the bird, felt akin to it—pursued by something sensed yet never seen. It was a feeling that made him want to hide. . . .

The dog was frozen on the grouse, frozen on the land. Time alone moved, ever so slowly. Bill saw the change in the shadows as the early sun inched down the brown hilltop to the north. He heard the murmur of the river in the low valley, felt a breeze brush his face and go on past to rustle the heat-beaten grass. He thought how nothing on the farm, in school, in his practice, or in any other aspect of his world had prepared him for this. Nothing had pumped him up, as a man on his way to the gallows, to look clear and hard at the world for the first time.

Recognizing mortality all around him, Bill's gaze stiffened because he realized he was about beat. Still, he knew he shouldn't let himself be. Fighting back was instinct, as much as the grouse's instinct to hide from its pursuers.

He was sick but conscious of it and alive and moving as a man on his way to town for the morning paper. But the thought of becoming forever what he'd never been kept coming back on him. Bill had dealt with various deaths many times before, yet never had it been his turn to do the dying. After nearly a lifetime of being in constant touch with people, he now felt altogether alone. And he felt burdened with this aloneness, this private pain.

Bill thought back to the evening when he and Hannah had arrived in Heathrow exactly a year ago. They'd stopped in their unpacking and had gone out onto the weathered porch at dusk. As their shuffling ceased, evening sounds gathered. A whippoorwill started its lament on the hillside behind them. The crickets grew almost deafening in the tall grass that swayed from side to side along the edge of the barn. And the coyotes resumed their urgent, evening talk above the aspen stand that ran from the high pasture on up. As dusk settled in over the dry hills, the land itself breathed. Bill and Hannah had sat hand in hand, scarcely daring to breathe while rocking to the peace, for the first time relieved and refreshed by finally doing something strictly for themselves.

Now as this peace was becoming so undone, Bill loved Hannah with a conviction that twisted and tightened him inside. He knew he must immediately dismiss this emotion to go on.

He felt the stirring of autumn, the long wedges of geese high in the clear sky, headed south. He saw the new dog locked before him, drunk on bird scent and sweet mountain air. He'd miss the cozy, clear nights when he and Hannah studied stars, safe and sound. Good Christ, Hannah. The thought choked him quicker than cottonwood snow in a spring wind.

Then Bill closed his eyes and smelled spring—all the water running down through this otherwise dry country. And the warm rains moistening the huge garden of earth, when the aspen budded out in stages into the hills and the balsam roots began to bulge and the air grew ripe with sage to the music of geese on their way north.

Bill studied the land before him and loved it as if it were his own. Not that he was indigenous to it, but it *was* his land, as he felt indigenous to all land right then. An ancient thing came upon him, unabridged and of its own accord.

A ray of sun rounded the hill and caught on the sage that the grouse hid under, turning the brush olive blue, and the grass before it tan. The hawk twisted up, caught a new current, and disappeared. The grouse shuffled from beneath the sage. The dog broke point and flushed it.

As the bird took flight, Bill shouldered his gun. He swung with the grouse and followed it as it sped away, crossing hard for the sun in the reaching valley. Bill followed it atop the gun barrels, instinct coming back through the years until he knew the moment was right to pull the trigger and send the grouse into a blur of feathers. Then he continued tracing the bird as it faded to a distant object, moving down and away into the aspen grove below. He eased his gun down and pulled the two unused shells.

Bill whistled back the dog , which had chased the grouse as any young dog might. He congratulated her on her fine point—a point that seemed to last a lifetime. And it may have, since Bill's measurement of time had become loosened as soon as he'd seen the hawk and the dog had locked onto the grouse.

He let his setter hunt up onto the ridge and then began following her back down the ranch side of the hill.

Bill once heard it said: A dream is a wish one's heart makes. But dream-time, he knew, is different than material-time. And it was more from his guts than anywhere that for the time being, he wished like hell to walk and hunt . . . and live forever.

The Wait

At 9:30 A.M., Craig's attention wavered. His stomach growled from thick coffee and nothing but the previous night's soup and pancakes. The hour-long drive had been an early one, and in the cold air he still wasn't rid of the rugged coffee. He slapped his arms to see if they were still there, smoothed the dog's head, and told the retriever that it could get up.

The Lab busted from the makeshift blind that Craig had scavenged together in the dark and bounded up onto the island. Leaning his pump gun against his pack, Craig stood to stretch. It was time for the cold pancakes with peanut butter and jam thrown between them—something that had looked so helpless the night before but now seemed like gourmet fare as he peeled them from plastic wrap and poured a cup of hot chocolate.

Once again he kind of wished that he had cut the stuff with schnapps. That's what "the old boys" did to ward off slow shooting—or so he'd heard. But somehow Craig couldn't bring himself to do it, not while gunning, anyway. The hunting rush was intoxicating enough, and he savored it for the reality it was. He knew that if he had stayed home and gunned his favorite local bog he would already be eating a big breakfast and would have mallards hanging in the shed. But he'd opted for the big water today. Big water meant big bunches of birds, made from about every variety in the book. Though the trip had been slow as he dodged road-bound deer in the dark December fog, the reward was just listening to the symphony of ducks somewhere out there in the dawn. The whistle of wigeon, the raspy talk of divers.

None had swung closer than fifty yards, and Craig wasn't about to break the cold and quiet for that. He remained content to sit behind the bushes on a recycled drywall bucket with his young Lab, which stayed intent despite not a shot. Craig watched clumps of mist skitter across the water like ghost dancers in some strange theater and knew that the best still lay ahead.

A thick layer of frost gathered on the turned-over canoe, the decoys, and the worn, brown L.L. Bean jacket that Craig had saved lawn-mowing money to buy many years before. The sleeves were now too short, and the coat wasn't nearly as weatherproof as it had once been, but he had carried his first birds in it and sometimes liked to sit shawled in its memories.

He waited for an old fog to lift from a tired piece of water, with a new kind of dog next to him and all six birds to collect. The hot chocolate in his Thermos was tepid, but it worked to wash down the overloaded pancakes and to push back some of the zero-degree chill. Craig felt the glob of sourdough steadying his hollow stomach. The dog came back to the blind with a stick—happy to have gotten up for a trot to piss on things. Craig was tempted to play with the Lab for a minute, but he thought better of it when a pair of big canvasbacks swung over the decoys twenty-five yards out. Naturally, having sat at red alert for three hours, he was caught away from his gun by these first birds.

He whistled the dog close and sat again on the cold bucket, thinking that his favorite times doing this were those when he was alone with the Lab. There was no one to answer to for a lack of birds, cold water, or missed shots. It was only the two of them, and the surroundings met their own desires just fine.

Craig remembered the early-morning geese that had sounded close enough to reach and touch through the fog. And the eagle that had caught a feeding widgeon and then smashed it against the rocks. And the salmon and steelhead that had poked their noses up into the breaking dawn. As if those memories weren't enough, just then flocks of waterfowl started to lift off the water and move again.

They started from a spot a quarter-mile downriver, in a way Craig knew they'd likely make shots. At first, always at first, it was hard to tell if the black-cupped shapes were coming or going. Till they grew and grew, and Craig sank in the blind and could see them heading straight at him. He worked over in his mind the color differences between redheads and scaup because he knew when they broke the point there would only be a second to decide.

The first group came on, and he couldn't tell whether they'd split or all go left or right. If they kept their line long enough, he'd have them either way. The outer fringe of the flock swung just shy of good gun range; Craig wanted to shoot but held off for the last of the bunch, which were still headed straight. As they broke, he stood and swung the pump gun. Redheads at thirty yards and sixty miles an hour. Craig missed twice, his young Lab bursting from the blind, only to be called back quickly.

He'd barely reloaded when another group of ducks bore down on him, his shots having stirred them from downriver. Craig could see that these birds, too, would make shots as they lined right at him. When they were twenty-five yards out, they lifted up, wings open, and he missed twice more. His young dog whined softly.

Another flock of divers followed. The closest bird swung at about forty yards, and Craig again passed on them. Then it was quiet. He swilled the rest of his hot chocolate, checked his shell box, checked his gun and checked to see that all the decoys looked clean. He patted the dog and felt his second wind stir.

Suddenly, from behind him, a pair of widgeon appeared. Their wings were set, but these birds were turning a little farther out than he liked. Then another group of low, hard-driving ducks came upriver. They would make it.

When they split, the divers to the right were too far, but the rest swung out front at thirty yards. Craig fired once and missed, then with his second shot he crushed a flying object and all went still as the bird fell, suspended. It seemed that a speeding sky raced on to leave the duck behind. Drifting feathers exaggerated the gun's complete connection with the redhead, which splashed feet up. It was a perfect shot that had been planned no differently than all the misses.

In an instant, the Lab was swimming toward the bird. And if Craig had been forced to wait all week, seeing his young dog come back with the fat redhead made it worth doing countless times over. This was what he had dreamed of since his older dog had passed on more than a year before. It was what he had anticipated all summer long. Now, nearing the end of the hunting season, he knew that all the training had paid off and that he had another duck dog and a new partner.

This was why he had come . . . that and to see these wild birds driving hard, right down his throat. Not the whisper of lazy mallards drifting into the decoys, but a roar of wings from a thousand divers that swarmed this mighty river like bees. To connect with one was to stop the world entirely, to meet a rare object from the realm of water and sky. Breaking something that was perfect in not being broken was at times a sad accomplishment but an accomplishment all the same. And what Craig felt most, over and over, was himself swinging the gun and squeezing the trigger and watching the shape of the duck go immediately odd. This was the strange occurrence that kept him alert for hours under a slow fog, just as he had been at daybreak. At any moment something big could happen in this solitary shooting world.

The next birds to break the point were fat greater scaup. Three shots left two drakes belly-up just beyond the decoys. Craig directed his Lab to the farthest bird first, then to the closer one. The dog refrained from trying for both in one mouthful.

Craig and his Lab had barely settled again when a single wigeon snuck up from behind them. This time he was instantly up and shooting, and the bird crumpled into the decoys.

A lull of several minutes followed the dog's retrieve, and the Lab shook with a mixture of cold and anticipation. Craig had all but forgotten about his own cold hands and feet, though shake water from the dog froze on his gun barrel. His attention was on the verge of lapsing again when a big bull canvasback blindsided him and swung out over the blocks, then circled back toward the blind. When the bird's feet went down and it was about to land center-spread, Craig stood. The big duck flared but not in time to avoid its fate. The young Lab sensed a true prize and, after retrieving it, trotted about the island a minute with the weighty bull can held high. Craig whistled the dog to the blind and had his own chance for admiration.

In an hour, it was over: Two redheads, two bluebills, one wigeon, and the handsome canvasback all lay on the frozen rocks next to Craig's backpack. He and the dog sat and watched as more birds came over the decoys in earnest. After a half-hour, he walked up onto the island, rolled the canoe out of the brush, threw in the empty decoy sacks, and slipped into the easy river.

It was much more real for Craig to do things by canoe: setting dekes, picking them up after the shoot, crossing open water. In a canoe, he always paid closer attention to details. Things had to be packed just right for ballast, as the journey could be a dangerous one if the wind picked up and there was imbalance within. Everything took longer this way, but some of the best hunts simply did take longer.

Sitting at Craig's feet, the dog was the last thing into the canoe, and as the two started for the mainland, the Lab's look was one of adventure. The fog had quit the river by now, and beyond the dog's broad head, the bow of the canoe sliced the water just enough for passing. The world consisted of dripping paddle water filtered through the sound of wings, as flock upon flock of divers moved off the river and climbed high overhead, into the noontime sky.

Craig wondered were the ducks had come from. "Up north," was the common answer. But exactly where? What waters had they visited? Farm ponds, inland rivers, glacial lakes, coastal inlets, the grain fields of western Canada? Even more, where were they headed? Craig felt indeed fortunate that he and the dog had shared this brief time in the birds' epic journey. And he hoped that the questions they always raised would never be completely answered.

Woodcock: A Boy's Thrill

Crisp maple leaves
float an October breeze
ripe with northern flare;
the sweet smell of spent shells
an afternoon hillside
of poplar, thin birch,
frost-killed fern, and juniper
the dull bell working again
a whole world full and right.

After leaving the tilting farmhouse—
the endless woodpile behind
with pockets full:
jam sandwiches, cider,
a few No 9s and 10s.
To follow along broken walls
the brusque, witching nose
of Uncle Thad's wild-assed dog:
a statue to point
but ate every bird shot
lest you got there first.

That first bird
soft in hand and russet brown;
that curious bill
and deep, dark, sideways eyes
gone still
in a land shot with gold—
Uncle's pat saying
"What a great thing!
That bird the size of a *barn*!"

Then, barely big enough
to shoulder the single-shot
you trace his footsteps once more
into scraggly woods
at once so different—
so replete, clear, and close
the small bird snug in your pouch
that you see corkscrew up
trip, tumble over and over
and will . . . winter long.

Now nothing can go wrong
for quite some time
even back in school
when they jeer:
"Stinky farm boy!"
you'll slowly turn
all warm inside
and smile.

Retirement

Jack liked coming to this spot on the river because the bitter-brush came in tight to its even flow, and he could snuggle down and smell sage all around him in the dew of an early autumn morning. Other places to patrol were plentiful: the usual boat launches of state reserves and similar, easily accessible gunning haunts. But only fools would break laws in such handy places. Poachers would be in the discreet areas that lacked commotion.

Being a senior warden of the state game department, Jack was different than most of what he called "the new breed." And he had a little pull. On opening day he ran standard patrol—checking birds, licenses, lead shot or steel. Afterward, he liked to roam.

He walked the stony shores of the Columbia because he loved the epic journey of waterfowl up and down this mighty river, and wanted more and more to stay in tune with it to better protect what was left of the river's wild resources. Waterfowl had adapted well to the new environment created by the dams. They had actually flourished, using the orchards and grainfields and vegetable crops. Redheads, widgeon, gadwall, canvasbacks, and—of course—mallards and geese now swarmed the big water like bees. Anyone who spent a season on the Columbia could easily check off about every page of fowl in Peterson's guide. The river harbored nesting ground, food, and rest in a stretch from inland Canada to the Pacific. Man had perhaps shut down the fish, but not all the birds.

Early in the season Jack was cruising the shores of the Columbia when he first came to the hidden spot by following the occasional thump of a shotgun. The shooting was not at all steady, and there

was seldom more than a shot at a time, so it took a while for him to
ferret out the source.

First he noticed ducks working this secluded area. Then he saw
a small spread of decoys he had originally passed up as real birds—
in a cove tucked behind a rocky point separating it from the greater
river. He watched through his binoculars as the mallards continued
to work. Then he saw one abruptly fall stonelike from the sky and
heard a gun thump. A black dog came from nowhere on the bank,
lumbered into the water, scooped up the bird, and brought it back to
the brush line, where the Lab disappeared again. Jack slipped off his
pack, sat down, and steadied his field glasses.

Several flocks swung over the spread and some put down, but
no more shooting followed. He scanned the riverbank where the
dog had first emerged but couldn't see evidence of a blind or other
significant signs of hunters. Then he heard the calling, for mallards
again. A pair circled and set into the decoys that sat in the water-
cress, the frost still heavy on the surrounding grasses, making them
white on water. Ice had been broken away to mud, and Jack recognized that ducks themselves couldn't have done this.

He was about to get up and approach the river when a darkly
clad man appeared. Again, Jack couldn't distinguish from exactly
where. Through his binoculars he saw silver hair hanging down from
beneath a full-brimmed hat. It fell on the shoulders of a faded brown
coat that barely reached the tops of the gunner's olive-colored hip
boots. The man waded out and started with the decoys, two dozen
at most. He left two out, and after he'd sacked up the rest, he sent
the dog after the pair.

The black Lab had a gray muzzle—lots of gray. Jack could see
the dog breathing hard as it returned to shore with the first decoy,
then methodically went after the second. The man didn't seem to
speak but took the decoys and patted the dog on the head before
sacking them with the rest. He went again out of view then returned
with a side-by-side shotgun and a string of seven ducks. Jack

counted six greenheads and a canvasback. The man threw the sack of decoys over his shoulder and the ducks over that; the dog filed in beside the hand that clutched the long gun. The gunner headed up the bank and into the bitterbrush and sage, then north along the railroad tracks to no place Jack knew of.

His line of travel was precisely in the opposite direction of the road that Jack had come from, a half-mile away. The warden never took his eyes from the man until he was gone out of sight: decoys, ducks, gun, and dog. Jack hadn't moved.

The sun hit the river hard, and the frost started to loosen and glisten. The mist shifted around in the middle of the river, tossing and turning like a restless ghost before starting to lift off the Columbia and join again the hard, bright, eastern-Washington sky—another bluebird October day in the making.

Jack breathed for what seemed to him the first time since arriving. He tucked his binoculars away, pulled on his gloves, shouldered his pack, and slowly headed downriver to the south, where his game-department truck was parked.

He promised himself he'd stay away from the area for a few days. However, so near retirement, Jack felt the stack of paperwork on his desk wasn't necessarily for his attention. Or at least he'd earned the privilege to forego much of it. Paperwork seemed to be a product of the new breed, along with timed coffee makers, swivel chairs, personal-relations seminars, and scheduled work hours. All of which, in his estimation, kept agents from afield.

So Jack continued to patrol as vigorously as his not-so-young bones and joints allowed. All the usual hunting spots seemed stale to him, though—stale as the coffee-stained bullet reports he had to fill out on the rare occasions he used his rifle to put down a starved deer, shoot a car-wrecked elk, or kill a llama-eating cougar.

He checked hunters who had shot limits of lesser scaup while thinking they were redheads. He checked others who had little to show but empty shells. Some gunners had a mix of other birds, and a few had shot geese; fewer still had hunted strictly greenheads.

Everyone Jack checked was solemnly obeying the law—no excitement there. He was glad to see a couple of father-and-son teams; this heartened him, as did the goodly number of birds this fall. Living on movement and numbers, if not savvy, the birds survived the hunting easily. Jack knew it was of small threat to them, at least in the present day.

The first half of season was soon to close, and on the last day Jack returned to the spot where the sage smelled extra sweet and the shade lay in the cove and kept the grass white. He arrived at daybreak. As the light grew he saw the decoys, he heard a duck call, he saw mallards—always mallards first thing, working the pink mist. The river itself was a living thing moving somewhere out there, listened to but seldom seen. The birds worked, went away, then half the bunch peeled off for the cove. They settled with little hesitation.

Various groups of divers began buzzing the current of fog. Some scooted past the decoys; others landed. Then a small flock of mallards appeared around the rock point and set their wings. As they cupped and started to hang, he saw a muzzle flash, and a bird from the flock's fringe fell. Then a spray of white water erupted, and a bird getting up from the decoys tripped. The black dog emerged from the bank and headed for the far duck. As the Lab started back with the bird, Jack carefully traced its return, trying to catch the exact spot where it disappeared into the shore. The dog was gone too fast, however, and was just as quickly back out after the second bird—almost as if he'd gone and come like an otter from its den in the bank.

The quiet returned. Far upriver Jack started to hear thuds, and more birds began to move. The majority whistled past the cove as if it weren't there: divers, always bound either up or down. Jack knew the early mallards were shot or gone, and now there would be a wait.

The next birds to come were gadwall, and they came nicely. He was surprised that there was no shooting. Then a group of pintails came around the point and over the brush, the way the mallards had. They landed in the decoys. Spray erupted from the water when they jumped. A bird faltered, kept going, then was hit solidly a long way out—too long for a good hit, Jack thought. At least with steel shot. The black tank mechanically appeared, went out, and brought the bird back to the hole in the bank.

As the sun broke from the bluffs beyond then flooded the river, five mallards swung over the decoys, departed, and then came again to the lifelike calling. They landed, they sprung up, and two were left behind for the dog. The Lab no sooner back with them when some divers rounded the point and set into the cove. Two redheads were left behind, and the "seven-count limit" was etched in Jack's mind.

For the next two hours he watched in silence as different groups of birds worked the decoys. He knew he should be attending to the other volleys up and down the river, but he was mesmerized by the calling and the birds. For a panicked moment, Jack thought perhaps the gunner knew he was there. But he decided this was impossible, for he had come in quietly, crawling on hands and knees at dawn, and the man was well settled by the time he arrived.

Around ten o'clock, the hunter started the decoy pickup, again leaving the last two blocks for the dog. After he and the Lab disappeared to the north, Jack, too, left. He went back to his truck and headed on upriver to finish the first season with the crowd.

···

On the second-season opener, the most active ducking day of the year, Jack was busy in his routine. He knew the pressure would die out fast after the first day, even though the birds were really starting to show. Finally, a week into the second season, Jack slipped to the hidden cove early one morning. There wasn't any shooting. A week later he returned—still no shooting.

Another week passed and the river quieted. Hunting activity relaxed; the raw, gray days of November hunkered down; and birds started to collect by the hundreds. Shooting came again from the secret cove: one gun, one dog, seven ducks a morning on both Tuesdays and Fridays.

The season moved into December, and Jack subconsciously adjusted to the gunner's schedule. He was joyed to watch the hunt this way. The birds were active, the calls haunting, and the shots sometimes long and beautiful and certainly not made with steel.

The birds and the hunting were what first intrigued Jack about his occupation almost forty years before. Back when a game warden was someone who got that way by being able to shoot straight, climb most mountains, pack a garage-full of equipment on a horse, and break up a barroom brawl. A man who didn't hold to a forty-hour work week but always had time to take the neighbor's kid fishing on Sunday. The profession had gotten sloppy since then because of the development, the demise of wildlife of most every kind, the political struggle over resources, the antihunting regime, and—finally—the loss of the essence of the wild and what it all meant in the first place. Watching the mastery of the hunt again soothed Jack some. Good memories returned as the pleasure of being "outdoors" flooded him. He damn near felt like going hunting himself. It had been twenty years.

He knew he should go talk to this gentleman and warn him about using the lead, tell him that those days had gone by. After all, this was his job. But Jack couldn't bring himself to break the spell. There were days of wind, days of rain, days of sharp and clear air. On one snowy morning the gunner shot two geese that appeared out of the fog. There was no calling, just a quick left to right on a day that wasn't a "legal" goose day, and the dog in the water suddenly looked small against the dark shapes of the big birds.

As the snow started to collect in the high country, Jack got busy feeding elk, and this kept him away from the spot—broke his schedule. It irritated him a little that the younger wardens weren't taking on the feeding, which required a lot of shoveling and lifting of sacks and bales. Jack didn't so much mind the physical aspects of the task, but he thought it would do them good; so many of the men in the department, he felt, had gone soft. What the hell was he hanging around for anyway? To walk the Columbia aimlessly? To do the bird banding in the spring because he enjoyed it? Or just to collect his pension? Thinking about that money irritated him even more. Still, what bothered Jack most was that he couldn't be with the gunner in his cove.

Christmas came and went, and the approaching close of the duck season was January tenth. When Jack returned to his spot, the Columbia was a different river. The land was stark and mute. Snow lined the banks, and the ducks moved three times a day for feed now. The bitterbrush stood stranded above the snow. Raw breezes came with the shifting mist—the bluffs above the river a windswept brown, with the faint outline of wheat stubble beyond that.

The gunner took his six mallards and one canvasback, then waited. A half-hour passed. Some mallards flew low over the middle of the river, and suddenly the man started calling hard. The birds didn't react at first but he kept at it: a brassy highball that echoed up and down the water, clear as a church bell. He blew harder than he would have for sightseeing. He wanted these birds for real. The mallards didn't need in, necessarily, but they soon lifted and swung in a widening arc against the empty, cream-soaked sky. They worked the cove several times. The calling softened, got raspy, then stopped. . . . The lead bird committed.

Never before had Jack seen the gunner take a leading bird. Never before had he seen the man "up the limit." The bird crumpled and smacked the water. Its orange feet kicked at the sky, then went still. The breeze stopped. No dog appeared. Jack felt his heart quicken. He fought to steady his field glasses.

Struggling, the hunter emerged. He carried the black dog as he would a child: its legs around his torso and its head upon his shoulder. He carried the Lab to the water's edge and eased it down. He knelt and smoothed the dog's coat before he lined the Lab on the swirling bird, then gently sent it. The dog took two shaky steps and stood a moment. Jack saw the gray muzzle sniff the stiff air. Then with great effort, the Lab waded in and started toward the bird.

The next shot rent the silence. There was no spray, and when the dog's head lurched under, Jack knew the man had loaded a slug. The water turned dark around the dog as it rolled like an old log and started down, swept into the fingers of the huge river that was the keeper of so much life and death.

The gunner knelt again by the water's edge. He touched the river. He scooped a handful and splashed it on his face as he gazed skyward. Then all was again quiet.

At once, Jack—the game warden of thirty-nine years—wanted to hide deeper in the brush, to hide his embarrassment for being there. He felt naked. He wanted to see, but he prayed not to see. He wanted to somehow communicate. He wanted to run away and at the same time wanted to sit tight and take it all for the thing that it was.

After a minute or more, the hunter disappeared again into the embankment. Jack waited a very long time. His feet and hands were freezing. But there was no way he was going to risk the gunner's ever knowing he was there. Ever.

More ducks came. But there was no more shooting from the gunner in the hide, who had no face to look at.

Finally, Jack could take the cold no longer, and he began to slide away on his belly. Through the snow and brittle bitterbrush. Through the sage that months before had smelled so sweet that he'd wanted to roll in it, doglike.

When he got far enough away that he dared stand, Jack rose and walked quickly to his truck. The cab was as chilled as the coffee in the bottom of the tin thermos that sat on his dash, the one that he'd filled each morning in his kitchen going on four decades.

He drove slowly away from the river with no direction in mind, just cranked up the heater and headed into the gray.

Fire Road 1050

The old man said go to the end of Fire Road 1050, park, and then head west along the sidehill for a quarter-mile or more, "If you want grouse." A series of springs hugs the hill, he said. "Birds thick as yellowjackets just before the first frost. Nobody knows about it."

"You sure, Clayton?"

"Been that way forty years. Don't see why it've changed."

It's a hell of a thing to see someone who has long enjoyed life much as you do but is now no longer able. The outdoors, the hunting, a mind shot full of memory and knowledge—and a body that has finally caved in to live on in some sort of bittersweet suspension through one more autumn. I eased Clayton's anxiety with some smooth, straight rye. Maybe even pried him a little.

Few visited him in his house on the hill any more. Fewer still brought him such gifts or showed kinship of interest. I could hear him strain in the bathroom, then finally there was a little trickle. He came back out and leaned awkwardly against the door jamb. I rose to steady him, but he waved me off and found his own way back to the chair next to the stove, where I'd thrown in another chunk of larch.

Now that his legs had quit from fifty years of masonry and bird hunting, Clayton probably figured he'd share a little. Because I'd cut him firewood for the past couple of years, and loved birds and sometimes a drink, I guess I set myself up as a listening post. His wife dead, most of his friends along with his last dog gone, and his only daughter living on the far side of the mountains, Clayton was left to while away the days. Sometimes it killed me to think about it, but this evening we were both alive with bird talk. And when I began to see his eyes water—from whiskey or recall, it didn't matter—I listened up real good.

"No sense wastin' time huntin' that road, though it looks sweet as mornin' dew," he said. "Drive right to the end and save your energy. Walk dead west, bring some shells, and don't let the dog get too far ahead. In a dry year like this, that spot will be crawlin' with 'em. Just be sure and take it easy. Don't go more than a couple of times a season. Best spot on the goddamn universe. And . . . "

Of course, I never drive anywhere I can walk. It's habit. Especially after bouncing along logging roads for a solid hour. I drove by Fireroad 1050 twice before backtracking, reviewing Clayton's directions, then digging out the atlas. The numbers on the Forest Service post had long ago disappeared. I eased the truck up over the first culvert after turning in the hubs, and I crept on a little ways in low gear before deciding, screw it. Besides, the cover on both sides of the road looked grousy as a painting. Soon as I found a spot wide enough to pull a ten-point turn in the truck, I jacked around, kicked the parking brake, threw a big stone under one tire, let my Lab out, then grabbed my coat, double gun, and vest.

Grizzly Mountain to the north still held snow from two nights previous, and the leftover Harvest Moon of September hung slightly worn in the crisp, eastern Washington sky. I had come to hunt, damn it, not to drive around. And what an afternoon for it. Last night's frost had left the fir stinking in the slanting sun. The rose hips along the gone-dry creek looked like wilted raisins. Scrubby ponderosa pines suddenly had that winter appearance as if snow belonged to them. The jays were noisy and the thrushes were leaving the country as the chickadees returned. The air was still and the country big enough to make me glad to have a jack and extra tire, a sleeping bag, and some grub in the truck. I checked my compass, loaded the gun, and headed up the old road into the heart of it—and in no particular hurry.

A half-hour later I was warm with sweat when I came across the very fresh cat scat. I whistled back the dog, who had been working ahead in amazement at finding no grouse.

I knelt and put my hand to the scat. It wasn't steaming, but it looked empty and felt warm. I rummaged around in my coat pocket for the pair of buckshot shells I always bring along. Not that I'm so worried about becoming cougar lunch, but I love my dog and he might look just right to a hungry cat. I glanced at the tattered L.C. Smith cradled in my arms and wondered if it would hold together through two loads of magnum buck. But I decided to keep hunting, with both ears open and my eyes sharp to the sides.

Another grouseless hour later, I arrived, huffing, at the road's end. Clayton never said anything about its being *steep*. Maybe the old man was right—I shoulda' drove.

The hills above the road nudged timberline and broke into scattered ledges, just the kind of spot I'd head for blues. It was tempting; another thousand-foot climb and I'd be there. I studied the ridge line I'd hunt once I got on top. It looked rolling and mixed and promising as any. Maybe it was just that I didn't feel right getting into blues until the dog and I were three-quarters exhausted, out of water, and about to give up. This is why I always headed high for them. I was torn, but Clayton had probably killed more grouse than any man living, and though he liked to hike about all right, shooting birds is where his keenest interest lay. Some days, it wasn't always exactly that way for me.

I watered my Lab, then myself out of the sport bottle. I could just make out an old skid road beyond the final log landing. It ran west, quartering the hillside and running straight toward the distant peaks. I checked my vest, saw that I had the right load in each barrel, and pointed the dog ahead.

When the explosion out of the brush came from thirty feet to my right I suspected cougar, though the dog had gone straight past it. Too late for buckshot; I just swung the barrels in that direction and thought of all the things I'd killed with 1¼ ounces of No. 7½s. Then I saw that unmistakable coal-black hide and watched the bear lumber down through the brush. Elderberry, huckleberry, serviceberry—they were all here, and the bear had been plugging himself. Once I'd got my heart shoved back down to where it used to be and had brought the dog around, we commenced.

My Lab started getting hot a little farther up the bear-scattered sluice, his tail going in quick circles the foolproof way it does when he comes onto birds. I could hear his nose work like a snoring vacuum, in fits and starts. Good time to bring the Smith up to port arms.

The first thing I saw was a grouse's head poke up from the suddenly green grass. Then the dog stopped and the air was all full of grouse, with me swinging on buzzing shapes until both barrels were gone, along with most of the first flush. With the exception of a straggler, which I barely had time to reload for and was able to finally connect on after missing the first two easy shots. That made the dog relieved—his eyes about as wide as mine. Ruffs, all of them: a tucked-away family up at this altitude, birds that—until now—no one had disturbed. I held the fat juvenile in my hand, feeling proud as the very first time. When I pinched its crop, elderberry and green grass spilled out like some tossed, wild salad. I let the dog have one more sniff and laid the bird in the pouch, where it gave that reassuring, warm weight that confirmed we were, indeed, hunting.

Silence followed the big flush, the kind of silence that must be honored by any keen grouse hunter because he knows the birds haven't gone far, that they can all see and hear him. He knows that they may sit or fly at any moment and that there is no damn way in this world of knowing which. Now, it's all dog work, and the dog is head-up and ready to get after them.

Clayton was right; this place was a haven, by Christ, up on this mountainside where the afternoon sun seeped in through the lush run of aspen and fir, giving the land immediacy. It was a garden on an otherwise dry landscape. I motioned the dog on with an easy voice, following as if I was walking on glass. I could hear the trickle of the first spring under the shade of thick grasses. Then the dog had a grouse flushed out of a tree, and it was headed right at me. I swung around to take the going-away shot but waited too long for the bird to line out. It was lost in the trees by the time I fired. The dog came back to check. Finding nothing, he moved on. This was the way of it through two more flushes, the way with ruffs: good sound, good hope, yet foliage that was too tight and shots that weren't worth a nickel.

Once we got past the point where the family of birds had dispersed, we sat, rested a minute, and gazed out over the quiet land below—so quiet that the shadows of the far peaks seemed to echo the way they only do in the fall: sensuous, smooth, full shapes of deep purple, the high larch turning all orange and white snow coming fast down the ridge lines.

Around the next sag in the trail the dog got hot again, then stopped. A huge grouse flushed and headed for the broken timber to the right. I caught him with the left barrel just as he was about to swoop up to perch. My Lab brought back one of the biggest blues I've ever seen, all as big as a barnyard rooster. The bird was stuffed with snowberry, and it dwarfed the ruff in my pouch.

In a hundred yards, three grouse got up and landed in the trees. When I got up to the spot of the flush, one rocketed out from overhead and swooped down through the fir.

Out of habit I made a poor snap-shot at a fleeting shape and got the expected results. The dog didn't even bother to check, moved on toward the clearing, and froze up. I hastened ahead, not bothering to reload my right barrel. I reached the clearing just in time. The dog went in and flushed two big blues. One bird cut uphill, the other flew downhill. I traced the sloping bird as it glided out over the old cut and crossed what seemed like a mountain range in its passage. And just when the mountain backdrop broke away and there was nothing but bird and sky, I pulled the trigger. The bird folded, falling down, down, and down. The dog saw all that and seemed, by God, impressed. He wasted no time in busting down through the slash to find the prize.

There are days—though not many—when a three-bird limit isn't enough, but today was one of them. That fast, we were done. Forgotten was the long walk up here and the lack of birds the whole way. Forgotten, too, was the fact that we could have driven to within twenty minutes of here. Right then, I knew why we had walked. Now, we took those steps in the good direction, with a full pouch and the fineness of the season, the beauty of the afternoon, and the rightness of being in such a place alone with a good dog. Things Clayton had surely felt here. The kinds of things we can perhaps take with us.

After cleaning the birds on the tailgate,washing them in the stream, and giving my Lab some goodies, we loaded up and started our hour-long bounce away from Fireroad 1050. Once on the main road, I headed straight to my house for the last of the sweet corn, dug some potatoes, and headed up to Clayton's for sunset.

He was slouched in his chair next to the stove when I walked onto the porch. A copy of the *Farmer's Almanac* lay sprawled on the floor next to him. I stood silently and peered in at him, sleeping. His face was drawn and his thin hair was askew. His flannel shirt was torn, dirty, and patchless, unlike his trousers, which were crumpled and spliced in both knees. He slept peacefully. The reflection from the sinking sun hit his picture window and spilled a long stream of orange light across the dusty floor to the foot of his rocker.

In the fall of the year, heartbreak can unravel from any given countryside. In the fall of the year, pain can be calmed to sadness and sadness to some sort of deep and quiet understanding that not all will ever be understood. It is the season that's best for living while you slowly fade away. For the longest moment I stood on Clayton's porch with a sack full of filleted grouse and vegetables and whiskey. I felt honored as hell to have what I assumed to be so many healthy years ahead of me. I hesitated to turn the doorknob but figured Clayton would want to have a sip at sunset and would be glad for the news.

"Gonna' be cold this winter, Clayton?" I queried upon waking him and setting the sack on the counter.

"Be a change if it ain't," he huffed. "Glad for the woodpile—even if I didn't cut 'er myself."

"Went up there today," I said.

"Any birds left, Bernie?"

"About as many as when I got there."

"You git' any?"

"Enough for dinner. Anyone ever bring you grouse for dinner before, Clayton?"

"Why, can't say as they have."

"Well, I'm proud to be the first."

We split the three grouse between us, washed them down with some clean rye, and soon Clayton resumed the woodstove position. And that is where I left him when I stepped into the cool, dark night with just a couple of leftover crickets trying to sing a lullaby.

The last thing I promised Clayton before I left was to keep Fireroad 1050 in the very best of shape. Grouse garden that it was, I'd only visit to see how things were growing. And maybe to do some occasional thinning so that the old man and I could share a meal, perhaps a drink from time to time, and lots of bird talk. Damned as fate is, he'd probably live another couple of years.

The Labrador

He is the old kind
Solid head, barrel chest
Thick legs to webbed feet
Before the field-trial lines invaded

Before duck dogs became rubber-duck dogs
When the marsh and ocean and November winds
Stirred that magic mix
And just being out there enough
Kept the retrieve in the retriever.

This is how I see him
Closer to ten years now than nine
Still full of conviction, of stamina
Seasoned only with the seasons
As I cast him out.

Out to mighty waters
Out toward a fallen bird
That he never saw hit
Much less collapse
Its dying taking a quarter-mile.

"Isn't that too far?"
Our partner's remorse or concern
(He had done the shooting.)

"Can he swim that distance?
Even if he does see the bird?"

"What do you mean?"
"Think he's going to drown?"

The Lab searches for a hundred yards
Then turns for me
"Back. . . . Back!"
A thrown-up arm
A steady voice.

He keeps on
Nothing but cold, flat water
The crisp December afternoon sun
Shining just so
That we may see
A curled and drifting duck.

Farther out
The dog turns once more—"Back!"
And then digs in
Into a different time
When fowl poured through
The Strait of Belle Isle
And men tested the early ice
With pick-poles and ropes
To shoot hundreds a night
Under the "lamp of the poor."

Careful, one must remember
For the Lab shares the same faith as then
The same heart and

May not quit at the word
Thrusting his head up in search
Well beyond earshot
"Dead bird. Back!" the last sounds.

He knows returning empty
Has been accepted before
Yet because he has made complete
Hundreds of times
Just in this lifetime
And doesn't know disappointment
He spots the bird.

Oh my.
In the waning chrome light
On a winter-quiet Columbia
He finds the mark
And locks on
So far from home waters yet
At home in every water.

I see the moment
Only a moment before
Hope is lost, regret realized;
His head the size of the other speck
We've been keen to watch
At once gains speed
A hastening vee on glass
At last rising up until we can *just* see
Gotcha.

I've lost track of minutes
Our partner shakes his head

My pacing lines
Across slippery stone
Past hanging willows
To where I'll greet the Lab down-shore.

A wake no more
His broad head growing
Turning again to laid-out ears
Flat upon the surface
And unwavering eyes
All calm, rounded
By the heavy bird
Gentle in his jowls.

The Lab's *seeing* me
Is what I'll forever see
Through the currents of my mind
The salt of my eyes
The spate of my maritime blood.

Chukar Hiking

The thing about chukars is they're not only ventriloquists, but they understand the human language, too. If ever there was a game bird that sought revenge on its pursuers, this is the one. And never was truer the phrase: "A bird in the hand . . ."

Take last December, for instance. Longtime expedition partners Mr. Chew and Mr. Tuckerman were returning from a fruitless pre-Thanksgiving ducking trip to the potholes of the Columbia Basin. Zero-degree weather had frozen most of the area they'd hoped to hunt, and two feet of snow had hurried the "grand passage" of mallards on their way south. Chew and Tuck had left after a third pathetic morning, despite another storm that promised warming temperatures. Now—hesitantly, if not glumly—they were making their way back north through some bleak-looking, overcast country, thinking of Tuck's warm house and picking on the Columbia River itself.

All of a sudden Chew innocently said, "Hey, what's that bird there beside the road?"

When Tuck saw it, he slammed on the brakes, which threw the burdened Subaru into a fishtail and woke the dog. Then recognition flooded him: "A chukar, of course!" he said. No sooner had Tuck spoken, when two more of the partridge appeared just ahead.

"Cripes, Chew, they're eating the sand left from the plow trucks. Poor buggers got driven down by the snow." As Tuck looked about, he saw nothing but prime chukar country: steep bluffs that stairstepped up and up to Christ knows where.

Now, Tuck never claimed to be a hard-core chukar hunter over the dozen years he'd lived in the West, but he'd spent enough time at it to have full respect for the bird. He recalled hiking five hours on his first chukar hunt before he ever saw a bird; two more hours before he killed one. He had taken a fleeting Hail-Mary of a shot out of fright more than anything, as the covey flushed and flew back down the thousand-foot cliff he'd just spent all afternoon climbing.

Most of the wild chukar hunts Tuck had experienced since then had panned out about the same. But somewhere he'd heard you could "really get 'em" when it snowed. "They'll bunch up more, hold tight, and you can track 'em."

Tuck and Chew had the snow all right (little did they know that the two feet on the ground was just the beginning). And when they spied a Department of Fish and Wildlife sign on the next fence post, Tuck grew hopeful for the first time in days. Soon he found a pull-off—unplowed, untracked—and was able to punch through in the Subaru. As he did, a covey of chukars flushed.

"Hell Chew, this is gonna be a cinch," Tuck said, fumbling to open up the back of the car, which was stuffed full of wet ducking gear, the alarmed Lab piled on top. "We'll have our limits in no time. Be back to my place for chukar din-din."

Neither Tuck nor Chew had brought appropriate hiking apparel: sturdy boots, lightweight poly clothes, water bottles. But Chew had thrown in his side-by "Sweet 16," and Tuck at least had the foresight to bring some No. 7½'s for his custom-shaped 870 pump gun. He failed to locate the open choke tube to screw in but figured it'd be pick-and-choose shooting anyway, so he went with the rusted-in modified tube.

"You ready Chew?"

"Waitin' on you dearest, like always."

"Ha, ha. Gonna be a piece of cake."

Fresh partridge tracks were everywhere in the new snow. Chukar talk came from above the two hunters and from ahead of them, too. Then up went a covey from at least two hundred yards in front. Brimming with confidence from what everyone had said about "easy chukars," Tuck didn't let this wild flush faze him one bit, and he told Chew to walk one side of the gully, the dog in the middle, while he skirted the other side. In full duck hunting attire—wool pants and heavy coats—with not a bite to eat or a drop of water on them, they pushed on for a "quick one."

The Lab was happy as hell to do something besides freeze its butt off in a clammy duck blind and listen to disgruntled hunters bicker. But after ten minutes of moderate walking and no birds up, the dull thump in the back of Tuck's head reminded him that he owned perhaps more than his share of the Italian fire retardant they'd taken orally the night before in effort to thaw their wader-frozen toes. At once he was steaming beneath layers of thick wool.

"There goes a bunch," Chew yelled. "Headed across the highway to where those others are calling."

"Aw, let 'em go. Plenty more around here. Got 'em right where we want 'em, now," Tuck assured, and the two hunters headed back along the base of the bluffs toward the small lake.

"Jesus! You should see all the tracks on top of this knoll," Chew reported. "They're everywhere."

Just then a covey exploded from a distant place and flew straight *up* onto the first bluff.

Another thing Tuck remembered hearing: Chukars always fly *down* hill. So he maintained faith that he and Chew would slay them on the flats. In fact, he was pleased that they wouldn't even have to hike to scare these birds down. But why would they be going back *up* for now?

Chew worked more to the left, and Mack, the Lab, followed. They put up a small bunch too far ahead of them, but the birds cut toward Tuck on their path to their kin in the rocks above. Remembering that he had his fine, sawed-stock, taped-up duck gun, Tuck guessed forty yards, passed through the leader, and squeezed. Nothing. He pumped, then got a full connection and the ball of chukar fell, well . . . for a long time.

The sight alone of Mack bringing back that blue gray, knightly looking bird through chest-deep snow was enough to cause Tuck to momentarily forget his headache. But at the time, he failed to realize the full significance of this particular chukar.

"Hear 'em Chew? Down along the rocks there."

"Yeah."

"Let's go. Be ready, boy. Could be anywhere and everywhere," Tuck said, repeating their usual battle chant.

Mack ranged to the bluffs (aptly named) on Tuck's right, with Chew to the left, and they beelined for the distinct chatter ahead, which sounded uncannily like quick laughter.

"Gotta' be gettin' close," Tuck said softly to Chew.

Mack closed in on the imaginary mark that Tuck had on the sound, just as he heard the same ghostly chatter behind . . . no . . . up to the right of him. "Huh, that's strange," Tuck remarked. "Coulda' swore . . ." Just then a bunch of chukars flushed far to the left of Chew, then swung up and away, into the rocks.

"Boy. They seem kinda' jumpy," Chew said. "Wonder if they've already heard the music."

"No tire tracks at the pull-off," Tuck assured. "Not now or recently, near as I could see."

"Truth to tell."

"Let's make for the lake," Tuck said. "Then we better try something else." They were all too suddenly running out of good, low ground cover. Tuck glanced at the sky—about 1:30—then back at the car—a quarter-mile. Plenty of time yet, he thought.

When they reached the lake, more chukar tracks than one could count were trampled about in spots where it looked as if the birds had crowded together and, in concert, scratched up the snow to get at the bitterbrush seeds, cheatgrass, ants, and whatever else they could scrounge during this season of hunger. Then the boys heard more chatter from up in the rocks, and thus began backtracking while Mack worked a rocky area. Again, a covey flushed from football fields ahead and made for the higher climes.

"There," Tuck pointed. "I can see 'em running, Chew. See 'em? A whole bunch, up in the rocks."

"I'll be."

"Whaddya' think?"

"Sure wish I had something besides rubber boots to climb in. Looks kinda steep."

"Yeah. May as well give 'er a go though, huh? A little ways, anyway. See what it's like." Unlike his partner, Tuck had thought to throw in his old pair of Bean boots for après duck-hunt purposes. But, as usual, the chain treading was worn smooth as slate.

Tuck soon spied a small crotch leading up through the first band of rocks. "Tell ya what, Chew. Stay right here, and I'll go up and have a look-see. Might be I can get a little above 'em, then herd 'em down to ya."

"Okay, chiefie."

Mack and Tuck tooth, clawed, and daggered their way up through the opening—slipping and sliding on the greasy new snow. When they finally broke through, a perfect rock bench greeted them, running along the base of the next bluff. It looked good, too, almost pasture-like, and the place gave Tuck some understanding of why the birds might be so fond of it way up here.

Tuck and his dog commenced easing along the flat, figuring to flush the birds down to Chew. But Mack got birdy to Tuck's right, and next thing a covey flushed from beyond the higher bluff. Tuck stayed his course and walked the entire flat without further incident.

"Better come up, Chew. Looks righteous here."

Chew skinned his way up.

"See that opening?" Tuck said. "I'll make for it and see what's there."

"Okay. Wait. Hear that? Over there." Chew pointed down the bench.

"Impossible. I just walked that. Nothing. Think it was from above us?"

"Maybe."

Tuck began climbing again, wishing they'd brought a rope and maybe some pitons. At least some water and a peanut-butter-and-jelly sandwich. No dice. Tuck drove the butt of his pump gun into the rock to better his traction and soon broke over the top of the bluff to see much the same as before: another grass- and brush-choked chukar hangout. He started along it. In seconds, Mack flushed a covey that crossed to the still-higher rocks. It was a long shot, but Tuck snapped two at the closest bird—to no avail.

"May as well come on, Chew."

When Chew huffed and puffed his way up, Tuck asked him if he was warm enough; heavy sweat beaded his partner's brow. "Sure glad I wore these wool pants," Chew said, sucking on his wad of tobacco. "Always got woolies on when you need your Carhartts. And always got Car—"

"I know, I know. Pull up your skirt and let's go get us a couple of birds. You work one side of this flat, and I'll work the other. No whining."

"Okay sweetheart. Ain't thirsty are ya'?"

"I've only been this dry twice before."

"The first and last—" Another group of chukars exploded out of range and flew directly below them—to the exact spot where Chew had just been. Tuck managed a fleeting shot; it came up short, but kept Mack from launching himself after the birds.

"Piece of cake, huh?" Chew characteristically spit a dark streak onto the snow.

"Yep. Sure don't seem to be holding worth a—"

A single chukar flushed from Chew's side. He raised his double and almost shot, but at times, Chew could be more selective than Tuck. He could let fly with the best on occasion, but when a game was new to him, he generally preferred to get the lay of it before jumping in. It was a philosopy that only made sense, and Tuck was inclined to agree 870 percent. But Tuck had seen chukars be chukars before, and he was suddenly glad as hell to have his 12-gauge with the modified tube screwed in. "I've been taking those, Chew," he said.

"So I see."

"Hate to say so, but it may be all we get."

"They sit tight in the snow, huh?"

"Hear those over . . . no, up . . . no . . . where the hell are they? Should we move up one?"

"You go ahead," Chew said. "You walk that bench, I'll walk this one."

"Deal. Dog will be close by."

By the time Chew took a shot—out of duty more than anything—Tuck had easily shot half a box of shells with no effect. And when he saw Chew next, his friend was laughing like hell which, Chew was getting the notion, might be the main reason for chukar hunting. That and building some sort of thirsty appetite.

"What's so funny?" Tuck queried

"Wished I had a video of you and Mack sneaking around that rock, ass-deep in snow. Go it boy!"

"What are you doing up here anyway?" Tuck asked.

"I wanted to see how you were doing."

"Well, I saw some down on that ledge and figured I'd come over the top and get the drop on—"

"I know, I know—Mr. Sneaky."

"But they was *gone*."

"Lucky them."

"Yeah, well I wouldn't eat that," Tuck said, pointing to the handful of snow Chew was raising to his mouth. "You know what they say about snow not quenching your thirst. Only makes it worse."

"That right? Know what the Russian's say? Toughski shitski. Never was a fan of Tantalus anyway."

145

"Tantalus wasn't Russian, he was Greek. And if it wasn't for temptation, we wouldn't be after these little bastards in the first place."

Just then, they heard more chukar chatter, which echoed throughout the abandoned canyon like a hollow wind rattling bitterbrush. The two hunters did the natural thing and kept following the sound, like frenzied marionettes being pulled up and down.

Within a couple of hours Tuck and Chew had chukars scattered everywhere. Well, perhaps it was the other way around. The boys were dying of thirst, and Tuck was down to three shells. Chew had fired a few more times. Then from his game pouch, Tuck withdrew the one chukar he'd shot what now seemed to be a week ago.

"Wanta frame that thing?" Chew asked.

"Thinking about it."

It took Chew and Tuck till dark before they decided that they were indeed stumped. By which time they could barely make out the outline of the Subaru some fifteen hundred feet below the bluff on which they stood.

"Piece of cake, huh boy?"

"Chukar hiking at it's finest," Tuck said. "Now we just got to get to that car without further failure."

About this time, more chukars sounded off from . . . who the hell knew? As Tuck studied the snow-lined breaks that went endlessly on and on, yet held everything immediate, the unnerving sound of the birds reminded him of gloom spooks ringing the bell of insanity.

By the time he, Chew, and Mack got back to the car they were well out of groceries, drenched to the bone, and still had a three-hour, fog-ridden drive ahead of them to Tuck's place, with the hope that the steady knocking in the engine wouldn't worsen and thereby leave them for the coyotes.

"Sure wish we had the ole Chinook camper," Chew said. "Great for skiing and hunting tours."

"I know. Hated to part with it. Great hike anyway though, huh, Chew?"

"Oh yeah."

"That'll keep you in shape."

"Around dark there, I was wishing we had our skis."

"So maybe we should take a break tomorrow and try some skiing."

"Yeah, but let's throw in a shotgun, some pitons, and a climbing rope. You never know, we might just run into some chukars. And be crazy enough to chase 'em."

Bittersweet

Snow stings Lester's eyes as he walks from the truck down to the river. He carries just a half-sack of decoys, a pocket of shotshells, and pump gun. His Labrador trails him in the dark.

This is his favorite place. The river splits alfalfa fields here, and the Lab grew up farming them with Lester. This was one of their first hunting spots, yet they don't hunt here as much any more. On this season's final day, they've forgone the bigger river thirty miles south, the boat, and the huge spread of decoys. Instead, dog and hunter have taken to keeping the last morning simple by keeping it alone.

After crossing the shallow rapids to the far shore, the one the birds better like to land near, the two walk upriver a hundred yards. Lester tosses out the decoys in a horseshoe pattern, loads his pump, and settles back into the brush.

Shooting time comes slower in the storm. A trio of mallards pulls around the river bend and settles in about thirty yards away. The Lab starts to shake. Despite nearly four months of hunting, Lester, too, feels his pulse climb. Silence is all, followed by a small chatter from the birds moving toward the decoys. Lester is having a hard time distinguishing the drakes from the hens, and the birds swim on by. By the time shooting light seeps through the falling snow, the ducks have drifted back down again to the dekes. They flush when Lester stands, and his second shot folds a drake. He doesn't try for more.

The dog is in and back with the bird, and Lester lays it in the snow beside them, where one crimson drop of blood trickles from its bill. Silence returns, and the winter flow of the cottonwood-lined river moves on. The Lab starts licking himself dry, shaking now from the chill of January's mountain water, until the months of conditioning slowly begin to warm him from the inside out.

A pair of bald eagles sounds upriver, then Lester sees them glide across the open field to a distant perch in some tall ponderosa pine. He recalls having to chase them from the decoys on occasion. Coyotes yip on the westerly ridge. The decoys are becoming snow-laden, so Lester wades out and dunks the ones he can reach before hunkering back in the brush.

A half-hour passes, then a pair of mallards swings by, blindsiding Lester from upriver. He's too late in response to shoot, and they don't slow down.

"Sorry, bud."

Another half-hour passes when Lester hears a quack downriver, then spots a single coming around the bend maybe three feet off the deck and headed dead on. The drake coasts toward the decoys and he stands. As the bird lifts up and tries to back out, Lester solidly trips him. The dog returns with a second beauty, all dressed up in the finest winter plumage: shiny green head, iridescent blue wing patch, wavelike tail curl, and bright orange legs. Lester places him next to the first bird, which has already gathered a white coat of frost.

Soon Lester can sense a drop of cold working down his neck where his collar doesn't quite tuck in. His plan was to hunt just a couple of hours, then pack it in for another eight months and head for breakfast with his wife and child. It has been, after all, another grand season. His Lab stayed healthy throughout; friends came and hunted; Lester, himself, stayed healthy. A long season these days. Lots of different birds; lots of birds still. More memories and lessons learned.

Lester is caught in these thoughts, mesmerized by the snow hitting the cold, hard water and building on the bare cottonwood limbs. He is watching his Lab, who appears almost tired, finally. He's even starting to gray under the chin. Lester is about to say to him, "The time has come again," and send him for the decoys when he hears the geese.

At once, they sound close. Then Lester sees a small line moving over the field behind them and angling for the river. Their line will not bring the birds over the makeshift blind. Instead, they drop over the cottonwoods into the pool some three hundred yards below, past the rapids on the bend.

Lester chews on this a minute. He can hear the geese, perhaps a half-dozen, talking downriver. The dog tenses, his ears perked in that direction and his eyes unshifting. As with Lester, geese add that bit of extra excitement to a hunt for the dog. There is but one thing to do on this last day—on any day of the season, for that matter: Try'n sneak 'em. That fast, the end of the season is held at bay.

After leaving the decoys to pick up later, Lester and the dog slide back into the cottonwoods—back into the field—and start down toward the geese. The blizzard holds strong. Lester has only No. 3s, so there'll be no long shots. He thinks to himself: Maybe I'll have some cover, maybe not, depending exactly where in the pool the geese are sitting. To be sure we'll have the muffled quiet. Next to wind, snow is a jump-shooters best disguise and today it's going to be a good, old-fashioned sneak.

The stalk is a belly crawl that forces Lester to push snow and check every so often to see that the gun isn't caked as he shoves it ahead of him, keeping the barrel above the snow as best he can. The Lab is on his belly behind him. Lester doesn't have to look. He can feel the dog there as the Lab bumps his feet now and again.

A small stretch of olive and dogwood line the upper end of the pool, but the rest of the shore is just rocks and the bank is little higher than the water. If the birds aren't hard against the far shore, Lester thinks they might have a chance. He pauses and strains to listen: The gentle flow of water; the hiss of snow; then, at last, a goose murmur comes from just below the strip of dogwood.

Lester crawls back into the field, drops downriver some and realigns with the birds. They didn't sound far off. He wants one.

Lester and the Lab are soon out of the cottonwoods again and this time have no cover save a clump of olive trees just below where they had heard the geese. But the olive are mere twigs this time of year and the stalkers are soon onto the rocks with nothing more to hide them except the lay of the land, with forty yards to the river's edge. Snow is working its way under Lester's turtleneck as he pushes along, once again on his belly. His wool gloves are wet but his hands are still warm. His thick wool pants remain dry as a woodstove.

Lester covers about half the distance to the water's edge, shaking, when he sees one tall head rise. Where there was nothing but snow, rocks, and water moments before, now there is truth to tell. Lester freezes. The geese are too damned far—fifty yards, perhaps. The dog bumps his feet again; Lester feels the Lab tremble.

Everything stops except his heart, which feels as if it's about to come out his ears. The decision is either spring up and run, with the risk of accident on the slippery rocks, only to shoot wild, or try to flatten out more, tunneling through the sparse cover, hoping to close the distance. Neither is a good option, and whichever Lester chooses is likely the very difference between a big old gander or none at all.

Maybe the goose whose head Lester can see is the outside bird? He hears the others; they seem closer. The gander's head slowly goes back down to water again. Lester and the dog budge nearer. He and the Lab have made it another five yards, and Lester knows that the end of the stalk has come. He lies in the cold while trying to calm himself for a few seconds. Then he wipes down the ventilated rib by pulling the gun back into himself with one hand, while keeping his other wrapped around the barrel. He checks the action, then whispers "Stay" to his dog.

As if from the dead, Lester raises his head. His eyes instantly meet the goose's. It lets out one honk and the hunter is up. The rest of the birds are closer, and they're up, too. Suddenly the whole

Christly river is up and honking, and there look to be a hundred geese. Lester drives his barrel through the trailing bird as they leave the water and start past him. He leads it ever so briefly, concentrating on forgetting all of the bird except its outstretched head. The goose's white cheek rolls heavily when Lester pulls the trigger . . . and that's all. They're gone: a small, thin line of ghosts drifting off downriver through the falling snow, taking the season with them.

Glory Be. The Lab comes splashing back with a dandy Canada held high. Lester's stomach feels as if he just had a cup of mulled cider as he hoists the gander over his shoulder. He stands and listens to the hushed river a moment longer, before he and the Lab bend to the storm and retrace their steps into the trees, back through the field.

A small group of mallards springs up from the decoys upon their return to the decoys. Lester stands, watching the departing ducks, then reaches down, patting his dog and grinning.

"Next year's birds."

Gertie's Bird

Dawn broke cool and crisp, with a thick frosting all across the land. It clung to the bright-red maple leaves, on the browning lawn, upon the leftover garden corn, down along the apple trees, and—when daylight came—on the windshield of the '49 Willys Jeep parked in the barnyard. Soon enough, the sun would turn the sky blue and reveal the type of October day that sanctifies New England.

Inside the settling farmhouse the woodstove cranked. The kitchen smelled of fried bacon and burnt coffee. A lady in her mid-sixties sat at the kitchen table, snug in a creaky wicker chair. Using a flannel rag, she meticulously oiled down a Remington double-barrel shotgun from 1910. Her long, callused fingers worked in smooth, strong strokes with engrained efficiency. Her dry, leathery hands suggested a life of outdoor labor, as did her creased face and braided gray, whiskbroom hair. She wasn't overbearing in size, yet her broad shoulders and thick forearms and calves made her look solid as a chunk of granite. Her large, round breasts hung heavily under her navy blue cotton shirt as she bent over the gun in her favorite chair.

"Well, meathead, looks like a good day to do business," the lady abruptly said while getting up from her chair. She walked over and leaned the double next to the sink. "I'm curious as hell to find out if you've any sense under the gun."

At the sound of her gravelly voice, a dainty English setter pup trotted in from the living room. At eight months, the young dog was small for her breed. Where most setters have black markings—spots or patches—this bitch remained completely white except for her floppy black ears, with her flared-out snout carrying black as well. Her head remained round still, though it did give hints of becoming longer and sleeker with time. Her bright hazel eyes looked at things with sudden interest; her whole face overflowed with it, and her mouth was full of sharp, puncturing teeth she found ample opportunity to use.

Melissa studied the setter's chest and slender shoulders, then the rest of her thin, straight lines before stooping to scratch the dog's ear. "It's a right fine day out there, Gert," she softly said. "I'll bet ya Eastman wishes he could go with us. He'd be layin' aside chores today for sure. He'd show you a thing or two about birds, whether you had any brains or not."

The setter's eyes began to slowly waver under the steady scratching of Melissa's fingers. The lady spoke again to the dog.

"Where you want to go, pup? We got to get you on some real birds today. The scentin' ought to be pretty good when that ol' sun starts to melt things. Should we try up around the Potter Place? The birds may be sunnin' themselves along those walls. Course, we could go down across to McFarlen's orchards, but I think it's too early in the season for 'em to be in the apples. Apples ain't really kilt yet—not enough frost until last night."

Melissa paused. She gazed out the multipaned kitchen window while sipping at her coffee. She appeared to be studying something far away. After patting around in her shirt pocket, she pulled out a large-bowled, cherry pipe and filled it half full with a pinch of loose tobacco that she took from the tin sitting on the counter beside her. She struck a wooden match on the seat of her canvas pants, and smoke soon began to roll up from the bowl.

"Truth to tell," she said aloud, "I think we should try that old skid road leading into the big cut. Eastman always liked that area this time of year. Said they'd choose the wild clover and fern growing there over anything. I remember, too, their crops would be right packed with those greens. Look just like Christly silage. Seems though it ain't too thick up there yet. You won't be whooped so quick. There's some gooseberry up along that stretch as well . . . then there's the cut itself."

Melissa drew deeply on her pipe and stared out the window again. After a short spell, she looked down at the young setter. "That's the place for us, dog. Let me get my boots, and we'll go see if we can't make that Eastman proud."

The lady left the window-side, walked over and got a pair of dilapidated boots from behind the woodstove, then carried them through the kitchen and into the living room, where she sat down in a large cushioned chair. The boots were old L.L. Bean Maine Hunting Shoes about a foot high, greased until they were almost black and now crisscrossed with wrinkles. The rubber toes and tops of the feet were scuffed up badly, and the tread of each boot had come unglued where it met the toe. The overlapping of the heel and the leather topping was falling apart as well, while the chain-patterned tread of the sole was now worn marble smooth. The rawhide laces were broken and retied in several places, so that they now only drew tight about half of a boot, unless Melissa skipped eyelets. However, some of those were missing, too. The leather loop used for pulling on the boot and for wrapping extra lace around the top was torn completely off the right boot. All that remained of the L.L. Bean insignia was a small piece of light-colored rubber on the left boot's heel. It would be impossible to pass them for new, but Melissa pulled them on over her rag-wool socks like old friends.

"God, ain't they comfy," she said. "They won't shed a lick of water no more, but they're the best pair of boots I ever owned, Gert. Eastman gave them to me for my birthday long, long ago. Way before your time. Before Julie's time, before Belle's, and damn near before mine. I don't dare send 'em back for repair again. And a new pair don't enter into my figurin', so guess I'm stuck with 'em.

Melissa finished lacing the boots as best she could, then straightened and gazed across the living room at an old pine desk in the far corner. A stuffed ruffed grouse stood on the north end of the desk. The bird clasped a small paper-birch limb with the three toes of each foot. The grouse stood tall and could have been walking through the woods on its chicken legs, not hunkered down low with its head resting on its shoulders as Melissa had often seen grouse perched in trees. She admired the bird, large for its kind, with a glorious spread of tail feathers and an unbroken black band running across the tip of the splendid fan.

The grouse's head was held high and turned to one side, the tuft sticking straight up. Its wide open, bright eyes looked at Melissa wherever she moved about the room. The breast feathers were a shade of gray that reminded her of Eastman's old barn sweater, with a special outdoor look and a smell all its own. She got up from her chair and walked over to the desk. There, Melissa contemplated the grandeur of the grouse a little longer, then began to stroke its plumage as Gertie came over and sat down beside her feet.

"That was the last one shot over Julie," she said slowly, looking down at the setter pup. "Fact is, it proved to be the last one for Eastman, too. Course, we didn't know it at the time. You never do....

"If you turn out to be half the dog that Julie did, you'll be doing all right, Gert. Sure is a pretty bird, ain't he? Old Charlie Bootlegger up at the end of the road manicured that ol' boy. Eastman told him it was Julie's last, and having shot over her himself, I think Charlie did an extra special job. He ought to become a full-time taxidermist instead of just doin' it as a rainy-day hobby. He could stand to make some money, if he don't give up farmin'."

Melissa stared out the window to the right of the desk. "I happened to be along that day with Eastman and Julie, too. It was a cool, crisp day like the one coming on now. But it was later than this. Early November, as I recall. Apples had already dropped and rotted. We'd been stackin' wood most all day. Eastman said we ought to go for a little hunt seein's how there wouldn't be much opportunity left before the snow got too deep. So we quit the pile, got in the Jeep with Julie, and drove down to McFarlen's place.

"At the top of the orchard, Gert, we parked under the same apple tree every time. Except that day when Eastman climbed from the Jeep, he flushed a grouse that was sitting in that very damned tree! The bird took off high when Eastman opened the door, but Julie never batted an eye from the back seat. Course, she couldn't really see any more and had already lost her hearing. But once Eastman got out the Remington and his vest and let Julie down, she started hunting along the southerly edge of the apples. We followed her for a half-hour or more, resting along the way, before she struck scent clear at the bottom of the orchard. And when she did, she swung hard to the west and started circling off slow and easy, the way she always did when she'd located a bird. Eastman used to say that by circling the way she did, Julie actually mesmerized the bird. She'd go round and round, closing the gap each time. As much as he'd like to have taken credit for this circling trait, Eastman said it really were somethin' she'd learned on her own."

Melissa paused momentarily in her dissertation to see if she was keeping Gertie's interest. She saw that she was and, so, continued.

"Ayuh. That circling got the best of that grouse soon enough because Julie's bell quit of a sudden and she locked tight, pointing hard back up the hill, every muscle of her broke body stretched tight as a clamped vice. And we just stood there gawking in the silent, late-afternoon sun. The only sound on the entire hillside was the thawing of the crusted snow, now soft enough not to crunch underfoot.

"Finally he spoke to Jules, a soft 'That-a- girl.' And I remember my heart started a-poundin' the way it always did when Eastman moved in to flush. He walked slow and steady up around front of Julie as if mesmerizing the grouse his own goddamn self! Then the big bird burst from a couple of feet ahead of Jules and in a gray streak cut toward the pine stand below the orchard. Right then I feared Eastman had missed him, Gert. He did with the first shot, but that tight second barrel caught him, by Jesus, just as that bird thought he'd made the pines. Julie never quivered. In fourteen years she had never quivered, and she stayed steady right to the Christly end."

Melissa took her time out the window again, looking down upon her own little apple orchard. She appeared to be searching hard for something—trying to recover some resolution she might have misplaced. Eventually she dragged her eyes back to Gertie, who still sat at her feet listening with the same intent she put into everything.

"And there he sets, Gert. Damned thing looks like it's about to strut right off that branch and jump to the floor any second! Yep. And now it's your turn. You're one from a long line. I don't know if you've got the makings of your grandmother or not. Eastman seemed to think ya did. That's why he picked you. That, and your all white marking. He claimed with his eyesight getting worse by the season, an all-white dog would make for easier spotting in the woods. Course my eyesight ain't failing—just my mind."

Melissa left the window-side. She walked across the room to the far closet and swung open the door. The closet had the mixed, poignant odor of deep woods and cow dung. She paused upon opening the door, as if to drink in that odor a moment. Then Melissa started pawing through assorted outdoor clothing within, until she came up with a tattered brown hunting vest, its pockets weighted with shotgun shells. She bent into the closet again, feeling around for a cardboard box in the corner. Gertie trotted up behind her and nosed her in the rear. "Hi Gert," Melissa said. "Don't get impatient, I'll find your bell and whistle. Got plenty of No. 8s, too. Don't suppose we'll need too many today, though. If you have one good point I'll be both pleased and surprised. Let me grab you a handful of biscuits and go give the cows their water. Then we'll be on our way."

Melissa returned to the kitchen. She dug out some dog biscuits from an overhead cupboard, threw a bunch of maple and birch wood into the stove, and picked up the Remington. Vest thrown over one shoulder, shotgun in the other hand, she left the house and headed down into the barnyard with Gertie bumping at her heels.

The feeling of finding herself suddenly alone in the world was a feeling Melissa had brushed with only twice that she could remember. Once had been about two weeks after Julie's last hunt in McFarlen's orchard that amber November afternoon. It was then early December—cold and gray, with half a foot of snow on the ground. Eastman and Melissa had been getting in the last of the following year's firewood with the help of their workhorse, Dan. Julie had shown signs of failing badly the previous couple of days. Usually she got up to wander around as best she could on her stiffened legs, at least to go out and relieve herself. But she hadn't moved all day. When Melissa and Eastman got back to the house that evening after milking, the dog lay on her fouled blanket, shaking.

"Better take her in to Doc Pierce and get it over with, huh?" Melissa asked more than stated.

"Yep," Eastman replied. "But I reckon me and Julie is goin' for one more hunt, first."

"There's hardly enough daylight for shootin', is there?" Melissa had asked in a strained voice.

"Nope, there ain't. But it's just enough. We may find a bird down below the apple trees." Then Eastman headed for the closet to get his gun and then for the door, helping the struggling setter to her feet along the way. "Come on ol' girl," he mumbled to the dog.

Melissa made a move to go with them. "You stay here," Eastman snapped. It was then that she noticed the deer rifle in his hand.

"Now wait a . . ." she began. But dog and man were gone.

Melissa started after them, then stopped short on the granite doorstep. She stood and watched as Eastman, the gun clasped in one hand and Julie slow by his side, disappeared down into the small orchard. The land was tangy and still, the way it gets just before a snow. Julie's bell yielded the only relief to the silence: slow, fading, then gone into the deepening dusk.

A full hour after Melissa heard the shot down by the pond,

Eastman returned. Melissa sat in her wicker chair smoking her pipe, staring at the woodstove.

"Don't want to hear it," Eastman said when he entered the kitchen. "Couldn't afford no vet bill." He walked into the living room and put the .30-.30 back into the closet, then returned to the kitchen. He walked over to the counter and poured a glass of cider from a jug he'd picked up at the root cellar on his way back from the orchard.

Eastman rarely drank any cider. He saved it for special occasions only. The end of sugaring season being one of honor; the end of haying, another. Following the sale of a dog or after getting the year's wood in. Simple yet important marks on the calendar of their New England life. Christmas also qualified. Once in a while he drank a little for the pain in his back, the cider proving out as aptly strong medicine.

"Want some?" he asked Melissa. She nodded. With his back turned to Melissa, he poured another glass.

"How 'bout some supper"? she inquired.

"I ain't hungry."

Melissa, too, kept her thoughts to herself as winter settled in, as if in haste to engulf the little hillside farm.

The second time Melissa had felt suddenly alone in the world remained fresh; the hollowness still hung in her stomach most of the time ever since Eastman's death. It happened in late August, at the end of hay season. Melissa and Eastman were working hard to get their second cutting in while the good weather held. They were on the last load as the heavy August sun dropped toward the round top of Blueberry Mountain. After they'd pitched the wagon half full, Eastman told Melissa that he'd get the rest and she could go ahead in to fix supper.

Sunset passed and dusk began to creep in over the land—the sort of dusk that arrives after a humid summer day, posing almost as fog. Supper was ready, but Eastman had yet to return with the load of hay. Melissa walked outside, inviting Gertie to go along, and headed back up toward the higher pasture. She remembered thinking it odd not to hear the steady moan of the tractor. "Damn thing must be acting up," she had complained to Gertie. "That must be why he ain't made it in yet. At least this year it decided to go to hell on the last load and not the first."

Rounding the corner of the barn, Melissa could see up to the top of the rock-studded pasture where it dove sharply down toward the other side. She thought she could make out part of the wagon just on the far side of the crest. Something didn't look right in the dim twilight. Picking up her pace, Melissa passed through the break in the wall while Gertie darted back and forth up ahead.

As she closed in on the crest of the hill, Melissa could see that the wagon was on its side, most of the loose hay spilled out onto the ground. She ran to the top of the slope. Down the south side of the hill, the earth was all tossed about, and the International Farmall tractor rested on its back against the stone wall at the hill's bottom. Melissa ran to the shape that lay in the middle of the hill. Eastman's punctured and crushed body gradually heaved up and down, and then fell forever still.

Gertie started to lick Eastman's face, the way she did when he lay stretched out on the living-room floor reading, snoring, or just when his back hurt too much for him to sit in a chair. Melissa had only seen dead people in caskets before, and they were usually fixed up enough so it was hard to tell if they were really dead. It wasn't hard to tell looking at Eastman. She watched Gertie sniff his body, then lose interest and sit down beside him in a whimper. Melissa bent to touch Eastman's bruised face but couldn't quite bring her trembling hands to do so. She knelt and stared at his contorted, stubbled face with its empty eyes before taking out her handkerchief and wiping at the blood that seeped from the corners of Eastman's mouth.

In time, Melissa turned her eyes up to the scattered wagon,

then down to the rolled tractor. She reached for reasoning: Why? How? The simple little accident happened so quickly and with such little warning. That fast, a timeless routine had been severed. Confused and foreign thoughts raced through Melissa, and in the end her mind just went cold.

For two days the cows went unmilked, Dan the horse was unfed, and even Gertie was abandoned. For two days Eastman's corpse lay up in the pasture and began to bloat under the humid August sky. On the third day, Jerry Tuttle from the Crossroads Dairy, where Eastman hauled his daily milk, came up to the farm to see why Eastman or Melissa hadn't been to town. By then Melissa had come out from hiding in the house and had already been up to find Eastman at daybreak. The day was already hot and muggy. Eastman's body was gone.

In a way it came as relief for Melissa not to find him there. She didn't have to go through seeing him dead all over again, then burying him. Also, she was now free to imagine where he might have gone. Although she figured most likely a bear had dragged him off, she also felt that perhaps a certain mystery still swirled about these worn mountains of New Hampshire after all. The more Melissa dreamed of this mystery of unexplained events, the calmer she became about the uncertainty of Eastman's missing body. By no means did she put his death to rest; however, she did go back to milking the badly swollen cows, and when Jerry showed up she explained what had happened. "I understand wanting to take care of your own," Jerry had said. "It's no one else's business how we go about these things Melissa. Your thoughts are safe here. Let me know if I can help you with the milk. I'm always happy to run up this way if you can't deliver. . . ."

...

The thawing frost dripped off the barn roof as Melissa stopped and broke the skim of ice from the rain tub perched under the gutter. Gertie lapped furiously at the cold water. "Be careful, dummy,"

Melissa said to the setter. "Don't drink too fast, or you'll get a damned headache." Smiling now, Melissa rested the shotgun against the barn, slid the door open, and stepped inside.

Steam rose off the backs of the eighteen stanchioned Gurnseys. They all shifted, causing a clatter of chain and metal when Melissa entered the barn. Gertie clung tight to the woman's side, keeping Melissa between herself and the cows—her head tucked low, her tail between her legs.

"Still ain't used to them, huh Gert." Melissa made her way around to the middle aisle—the main aisle of the barn, which had fifteen stanchions lining either side.

"What ya gonna to do now, dog? You got 'em on both sides of ya!" Gertie skittered over to a pile of hay in the middle of the aisle and buried herself in it, leaving just her black ears, nose, and wide eyes exposed. She remained there while Melissa watered each of the cows with two galvanized pails.

Previously, additional ten cows had occupied the barn, but Melissa had sold them after Eastman's accident. She decided twenty-eight head were too many to clean, feed, water, milk, breed, fence . . . She sold the oldest and least productive to Davis's slaughter house in September. She hated it for days, but this appeared to be the only course that made any sense to her. The cash didn't hurt, either. But now a certain emptiness haunted the barn, at least the lower end where the stanchions were vacated. She sensed this void every time she walked by, just the way she felt Eastman's void most every morning she came down at 4:30 to milk. She knew, though, that the barn would always shelter stock of some sort. "You're never alone on a farm," she assured Gertie.

After the watering, Melissa swung open the lower door of the barn and started undoing the stanchions. She released the cows closest to the door first, then worked her way back, leapfrogging between the two aisles. The front cows milled around a little at the door, but the ones in back soon pushed them out.

"Come on, girls," Melissa said. The cows knew the routine, as did Gertie, who by this point had made herself even more invisible in the hay. As soon as the last cow was out to pasture, joining Dan the horse, and the door had closed behind them, the setter bounced up, freeing herself from the hay. While Melissa hoed, shoveled, and wheeled manure, Gertie ran around the barn as if there'd never been a cow in it.

"Brave soul, ain't ya," Melissa said to Gert, as she wheeled the last load up the ramp and dumped it out the large window at the high end of the barn. "Let's' go have a tour, Gert. I'll tamp that pile down some other time. Too nice of a day to be treadin' in the shit." With that, they left the barn.

The Willys sputtered at first, but after a couple good pumpings on the gas, the engine caught and hung on and soon raced to a high idle. "She's a good rig," Melissa said to Gertie, who sat on the seat next to her. "I think she even enjoys the cold sometimes. I know she loves to plow snow. Too bad that her frigging heater don't work. Suppose I'll have to try'n fix her before winter. That sun feels good coming through the windshield now, don't it, Gert? It's when you're plowin' and can't see nothin' cause of no defrost that she's tough. Eastman plowed straight on into that granite post at the end of the yard during one storm. He said that snubbed him up. Made his teeth chatter wicked, besides stavin' the front end all to hell."

Melissa eased in the choke and hit the gas again to idle down the Jeep before dropping it in reverse to turn around. Then she and Gertie were headed out the dirt drive away from the farm, the Willys purring right along.

Bird hunting was one of the few things Melissa and Eastman ever did together that failed to entail work. Fishing was another. And on very rare occasions in the summer, they might pack a picnic supper to the top of Blueberry Mountain to watch the sun set. Maybe once a summer.

Eastman had always kept bird dogs around, and they had been

English setters for years, all from the same line. He had bred as well as trained dogs for other people, too. Usually these were city folks, and generally Eastman never had more than a handful of dogs around at any one time. It remained a hobby, and he allowed it to go on as one because he was very good at it and got top dollar for his dogs.

Still and all, he kept humble about his dogs, even knowing how much they were worth to a "sportsman" from Boston or New York. He prided his setters as being grouse dogs. Woodcock were just as plentiful where he lived, but he used to say, "Anyone could train a woodcock dog." Eastman trained a few woodcock dogs in his early days and at times enjoyed hunting woodcock, as well. However, grouse intrigued him more all the time.

In the end Eastman quit training and breeding dogs for a number of reasons and sold his line to a fellow in Vermont, keeping one last dog for himself. That dog was Julie, Gert's grandmother. He hated to send a dog that had grown up on his farm off to the city. Chances were that the dog had hunted more in three years with him than it would the rest of its life. This had always bothered Eastman. Melissa used to tell him, "The dogs hate to see you go, as much as you do them."

These thoughts traveled along with Melissa's as she swung the Jeep onto the logging road. Though she had assisted Eastman with training many times, and had hunted with him as well, she had never single-handedly *finished* a dog. She realized Gertie's great potential; the last thing she wanted to do was cause her failure. She had made a silent vow to train Gertie well. As Melissa had said to the dog earlier that morning, she wished to make Eastman proud "wherever the hell he may be."

"Guess we're goin' to have to teach each other," Melissa said, as she brought the Jeep to a halt where a large oak had been purposely dropped across the road. Gertie sat in the passenger's seat, ears perked, not sure exactly what was going on but excited for adventure.

"So far, Gert, you've been real uncooperative. I know that Eastman started you, but by Jesus I'm going to see to it you finish. I wish the old boy were here, too. It'd be a lot easier on the both of us. Sometimes he still pisses me off."

Gertie's number of rides in the Jeep had been limited. Each time had been en route to a bird cover. Melissa had brought the setter out a handful of times during September, and the dog had found birds under Melissa's steady hand. However, Gertie hunted too fast and often bumped birds before she realized what was happening. She had only a handful of decent points to her credit.

On one of these September training sessions, Melissa became so frustrated with Gertie's ranging too far out and not listening for her commands, she broke down and beat Gertie. Eastman himself seldom, if ever, used physical force in his training, only with the most bull-headed of dogs. Melissa knew that he'd have been furious if he'd known. At the time, she didn't care. It was a long Jeep ride home that night, neither Gertie nor Melissa very sure of one another. The beating never happened again.

Beyond the fallen oak, young alder fast encroached upon the road, turning it more into a path. The alders stood head-high and stuck mostly to the road, quickly giving way to larger aspen, birch, and young fir farther to the sides. The fast-growth trees gave the abandoned road a thick border in most places. Deeper into the woods, past this barrier, the floor thinned out. Here maple, oak, and beech grew tall, intermixed with towering white pine.

The old road opened up more in some places, mostly where old log landings once existed. In these clearings, some a hundred yards wide, wild clover grew, along with fern and other greens. These landings were near the heavily and sometimes clear-cut areas that now held a mix of wild fruits: raspberries, gooseberries, chokecherries, thornapples, grapes, and more. The road stretched on for three or four miles this way, wandering off into the mountains and eventually ending in one large cut of some fifty acres.

Much of the logging here had been done by horses, in the winter, and by men with strong backs and even stronger constitutions. Eastman had been one of these men.

Melissa studied the road through the windshield of the Jeep, taking in the mixture of colorful hardwoods—the day so clear and perfect it made her almost uneasy. She should have no excuse for feeling poorly on a day like today, yet she wished it were a gray November morning instead. The highlighted beauty of the turning leaves she recognized as an illusion, anyway. She thought of how the leaves were actually dying; a big, red oak leaf drifted slowly to the ground without a sound. A gray squirrel raced across the felled oak log with a cheek full of nuts. "Gettin' ready for winter," Melissa said out loud, then added: "Already."

She drew a deep breath then let out a long sigh. She took off Gertie's collar, slipped a bell onto it, then buckled it around the setter's neck again. She pulled a whistle from the hunting vest and slipped it over her head. After stepping from the Jeep, she slid the Remington out of its leather case in the back seat, then clicked her fingers for Gertie to follow. She stepped across the log, Gertie leaped over it, and the two of them headed up the road.

"Good God it smells sweet this morning, don't it Gert? I'd like to have a dog's nose for just five minutes. The woods must be full of so many good-smellin' things it'd make ya crazy. No wonder that nose of yours is going all the time. Why don't you stick it in along the edge there and warm 'er up. Might be that you'll end up runnin' right up a grouse's patootie!"

Melissa motioned with her arm to the right side of the road. Gertie, who was struggling against herself to stay at heel, now plunged into the thick road edge and began working along, her nose glued to the earth. When she got some fifty yards ahead, Melissa blew the whistle once. Gertie stopped. Melissa blew the whistle again, and Gertie crashed out into the road then stood, ears perked, looking back at her mistress. Melissa motioned to the left with her arm, and Gertie headed into the thick stuff on the left of the road. She hunted back to Melissa and would have kept going on by, but Melissa blew the whistle. Again Gertie stopped short. Another whistle and the dog came back out next to Melissa on the road.

"Not bad," Melissa said. "I think you must have some of Julie's quartering instinct. Thing is, Gert, you're just like any other puppy when it comes to speed. I've yet to see a pup that didn't hunt at a hell-bent pace. Hardest thing to do is to slow a dog down. Birds would help."

Melissa bent and stroked the setter's head. "Now, eeeasy," she said slowly. Gertie stood tense as Melissa touched her. Melissa stood up, cradled the shotgun in her left arm, then motioned with her right arm. Gertie leaped back into the thicket and started working again.

This time, Melissa let the dog get a little farther ahead before she blew the whistle. Gertie stopped. Another blast and she reappeared in the road, then started working her way toward Melissa. About halfway back, Gertie stopped short—a split second before a grouse flushed. The bird flew out of the dense edge, affording Melissa a perfect broadside view of it crossing the road before thundering into the woods on the opposite side. Gertie followed the bird until she hit the road, where Melissa's sharp "Whoa!" stopped her as abruptly as a brick wall.

"Whoa!" Melissa repeated, walking up to Gertie. "Whoa, that's a bird. Whoa!" Gertie stood with every muscle cocked, wanting badly to continue in pursuit.

Melissa leaned the shotgun in the crotch of a nearby alder, then bent over and picked Gertie up. She carried the dog back into the thick where she and the grouse had come from. As she placed Gertie back on the ground, the setter's nose worked incessantly.

"Whoa," Melissa repeated, stroking Gertie's back. "Good girl. That's a bird, whoa." Melissa slowly exerted pressure on Gertie's rump, as if to push the dog ahead. Gertie resisted this pressure.

The more Melissa pushed, the more Gertie resisted. Melissa spoke calmly, repeating "Whoa." In time, she took her hands off the dog. Gertie now stood steady. "Good girl."

The woods were dead still with just the clear blue sky as a backdrop for a dappled landscape created by the dying leaves of so many trees. As the sun made its way higher into the blue, even the shadiest parts of the woods thawed. This cool moisture hugged scent to the ground.

Melissa and Gert walked back out to the road. They could have crossed and pursued the bird they'd flushed, but the woods were thatched with foliage. Though Gertie could stretch her legs out there and practically run underneath the thick of the woods, to shoot at a speeding grouse while standing in the midst of such a web of vegetation would be but a waste of a shell. Melissa motioned Gertie to continue hunting up along the road.

The setter moved on, quartering in even fashion from one side of the road to the other. Melissa had helped refine this hunting instinct back in one of the hayfields in September, using a long check cord. A quarter-mile up the road on the right lay the first of the old log landings. Gertie picked up bird scent early while approaching the upper edge of the landing. Her small body fell captive to her nose; Melissa could hear the setter working in quick jerks left then right along the bird's trail.

Until the musical sound of the bell stopped and nothing stirred.

Then, as suddenly as the bell had fallen silent, it started again. The noise of the working dog traveled to within five feet of the landing edge, then fell quiet again, buried in a briar patch.

Melissa barely made out a patch of white that she identified as Gert. Although she hadn't seen any of the hunt, Melissa had a good idea of what had taken place by the abrupt stops and starts of Gertie's bell. The grouse had run ahead from the first point and, somehow, Gertie hadn't broken after it but picked the scent back up and followed it to the very edge of the clearing. The bird was now trapped.The grouse's last resort was to take flight into the open, which would have defied all its instincts to remain unexposed. So the bird had simply holed up instead.

"Good girl, Gert. Whoa, you got 'im, WHOA." Melissa carefully made her way into the woods, coming in from behind Gertie. She talked low to the dog the whole time she was on the move, finally reaching Gertie before either bird or dog had budged.

"Easy girl, easy." Melissa spoke to the setter as she stroked her white coat and pushed the dog into the point as she had done before. After thirty seconds, which felt like an hour to Melissa, she clipped a length of rope onto Gertie's collar, stood up while still speaking to the dog, and waited. A blue jay pierced the silence of the situation, which now lay in the hands of bird and dog. Melissa waited on, captive herself.

What suddenly changes such situations Melissa would never know, but at once she caught a glimpse of the grouse as it stirred and took the two or three steps they always do before taking flight. The bird flushed and thundered out of the briars, into the open of the landing. Melissa braced herself as Gertie broke.

The dog crashed through the briars and into the opening in mad pursuit of the bird. She made it twenty feet to where the rope ended. Here, she struck an imaginary object and was jerked off her feet into a backward summersault, as if striking an electric fence. "WHOA!" said Melissa.

Gertie cowered as Melissa approached her. "Whoa," repeated Melissa, reaching down to unclip the check cord.

"You did good, Gert, right up till the end. That weren't nothin' I didn't expect. You'll learn not to break quicker than you'll learn the rest. That point were nothin' to be ashamed of, girl." Gertie tried to snuggle up to Melissa's leg as the woman spoke. They rested for a time, and Melissa lit up her pipe.

The day turned into an extended one for both woman and dog. They hunted into the mid-afternoon, eventually making it to the end of the road where the big cut lay open against the mountain. A fair number of birds along the road afforded some good training for Gertie. She had two more staunch points before reaching the road's end. On the first one she broke when the bird flushed. However, Gertie stopped on her own just before reaching the end of the rope—a memory flash that saved her from being jolted once again. On Gertie's second point, she remained solid and didn't waver even when the bird exploded.

The idea of Gertie's hunting for such a long period of time at her young age didn't appeal much to Melissa. However, she realized the day as a good one for training, and the farm might not let her get away again soon. She knew there was no better time to train the dog than when it was young and before it had chance to develop unfavorable habits.

The 12-gauge Remington had rested all day in Melissa's arms and without a shell in it; the gun's twin barrels remained broken open and collected only twigs. As Melissa and Gert worked their careful way into the big cut, Melissa dropped a pair of shells into its breech.

The year wasn't a spectacular one for wild fruits; nonetheless the overgrown cut still yielded a fair assortment. Eastman had filled many a stew pot with plump, juicy hunks of grouse breast from this spot over the years. Mixed with carrots, potatoes, onions, and other odds and ends, Eastman's stew couldn't be beat. Melissa had watched him and his dogs at this spot on many occasions. In drizzle, wind, snow, or sun, this was the place of places to shoot grouse.

Eastman had shared the shotgun with Melissa at times, and she had learned to shoot okay though she generally preferred just to watch—happy to be along with him doing something besides work. She enjoyed Eastman most on bird hunts. He had an unlimited knowledge of the woods and was willing to share it with her. It was the only time he talked freely with her, or anyone for that matter.

Gertie's bell fell silent somewhere in the tangle of grapevines, which ran for some hundred yards along the edge of the cut. In places, a few small maples struggled up through the vines, a result of a seed misplaced by a spring's wind or perhaps a futile attempt by some wayward bird.

Melissa waded into the waist-high vines, the shotgun held up in ready position. Forty yards into the patch she spotted Gertie, her white coat disclosing her location once again. Melissa now understood Eastman's reasoning in choosing Gertie for her primary color.

The setter stood locked up. Until now, Melissa had remained calm through the day: patient during Gertie's mistakes, encouraging during her points, and not thinking at all about actually shooting birds. Her heart now jumped a couple of beats, the way it used to when Eastman walked in on a point. And she knew she must do her best to shoot this bird in order to complete the cycle.

She waited twenty feet from the dog, letting Gertie hold the point long as she would. The mountainside was all quiet, then a flurry of action erupted. The grouse flushed up out of the tangle and raced into the cut. The gun came up in Melissa's hands without her thinking and at thirty yards, the bird died. Gertie never budged.

"Good girl, Gert, you're a good girl." Melissa stroked the young dog's coat. "You did *good,* ya little shit!"

Then she called Gert to a heel and they walked to where the grouse had collapsed at the shot. "Okay, hunt," Melissa said. Gert started hunting, then slammed on point.

"*Good* girl," Melissa said, bending over to pick up the dead bird. She held it under Gert's nose, complimenting her some more. One drop of blood ran down the grouse's beak. "We'll teach you to retrieve another day. But today you got your first."

They walked over to a beech stump and sat down. "Think I'll see if Bootlegger wouldn't mind prettying this one up in his spare time. We'll put it right next to Julie's. It ain't quite so big and handsome, but she's genuine."

Melissa patted the young grouse's plumage. Right then is when she noticed a similar pattern in the old sweater that was half buried in the leaves beside the stump. It looked exactly like Eastman's barn sweater. Melissa reached over and picked it up, running the sleeve through her fingers to make sure it was real. It smelled mostly of the dank woods but did carry a faint trace of cow barn.

"How in the hell . . ." Melissa started. Then she stopped herself. It *could* be as well as it *couldn't*, really, when all was said.

The sun dropped closer to Blueberry Mountain to the west and a near-full moon had already risen in the crystallized October sky. Smoke drifted up from the bowl of Melissa's pipe, creating long gray wisps of life that hung frozen in the fast-cooling air. She could feel the mystery of autumn, the way she had for years during this season. It remained an indescribable sense, somewhere between beauty and sadness. Her inability to identify the emotion once troubled her, but now she began to feel an acceptance drift in. After all, as Eastman had said about most anything he couldn't or didn't care to explain, it remained "just the way of it."

Melissa brought the sweater up to her face and took deep breaths of it, her hands not so steady anymore. She could see Eastman standing in the late October woods with his old green crusher hat on, his worn vest over this very sweater, his pipe sticking out one side of his mouth, the double gun at port arms, and a beautiful pointing setter at his feet. He was tall and thin, and very slowly he turned his head to catch Melissa with his eyes. Therein lay that irresistible twinkle he *only* had when all was right in the world . . . and that was when birding.

Melissa scuffed the heel of her tattered boot in the pile of yellow leaves. Were her eyes stinging from the cold? "We best get hustlin', Gert," she said. "I'm sure there are plenty more grouse in here like this one but we got things to do yet. Should've been back for milkin' an hour ago." Miles across the painted valley of pasture and woods a cowbell chimed; a cow, indeed, bellowed.

Melissa smoothed the barrels of the Remington cradled in her arms, tapped her pipe on the side of the stump, put the sweater back in the leaves, then stood up. She took Gertie's bell off and gave her another pat. "We did good today, Gertie. We did damned good." And they started back down that less lonesome road.